TRAFFICKED

TRAFFICKED

The Terrifying True Story of a British Girl
Forced into the Sex Trade

Sophie Hayes

HARPER

HarperCollins*Publishers*
1 London Bridge Street
London SE1 9GF

www.harpercollins.co.uk

First published by HarperCollins*Publishers* 2012

1

© Sophie Hayes 2012

A catalogue record of this book is
available from the British Library

ISBN 978-0-00-821955-0

Printed and bound in the United States of
America by LSC Communications

Find out more about HarperCollins and the environment at
www.harpercollins.co.uk/green

This book is dedicated to Jenna,
to all the other women, men and children
who have been affected by human trafficking,
and to all the people who have supported me
– and are still supporting me – on my journey.

Acknowledgements

For the first couple of years after I came home it felt as though I were living in purgatory. One man took away years of my life when I was young and should have been happy. I know I can never reclaim the years I've lost, but I *can* make sure that they become the foundation of a new life – for me and, I hope, for other people too. Everyone deserves freedom and basic human rights, and although he stole my freedom, I am going to do everything in my power to fight back and make a difference.*

The hardest part about writing my story has been the fact that, for me, it isn't just a story. It was my life – and something reminds me of it in some way every day so that I see images in my head of what happened, like a film playing over and over again. But instead of making me weaker, that reinforces the strength other people have helped to give me. I remember that I am strong and that I will not let him beat me, and this gives me the inspiration and motivation I need to be able to do what I can to try to help prevent similar crimes being perpetrated against others.

The amazing people who have protected and guided me since I returned to the UK have saved my life. They are the ones who have made it possible for my book to be written, and I want to thank them with all my heart.

It devastates me knowing what my mum had to endure. I lived through what happened, but she can only imagine it, and I'm not sure which is worse. My family have been my world; they have supported me and have never treated me any differently as a result of what happened. My mum and my stepdad are my guardian angels, not least because they rescued me from a fate that I don't even want to think about.

I was very fortunate to make contact with STOP THE TRAFFIK. Bex, particularly, became my lifeline when I thought I was going to drown; she has become my friend and my inspiration, and I will never be able to thank her properly for what she's done for me. I am also indebted to Ruth, Simon and the rest of the team at STOP THE TRAFFIK, who have become my extended family, and to the friends who have helped me to see things differently by showing me that there are amazing people in the world and by giving me hope that one day I might find someone who loves me for who I am. My friends have helped me to open my eyes, and for that – and many other things – I thank them.

I am also grateful to Robin – not only for what he's done for me, but for what he does every day for so many other people – and to everyone who works with him in the battle against human trafficking and tries to make a difference.

And I want to thank all the people involved in making my book a reality – my publisher, HarperCollins, Jane, my wonderful writer, and my agent.

Thank you to all the people who have helped and supported me, and thank *you* for reading my story.

*I have recently set up the Sophie Hayes Foundation (www.sophiehayesfoundation.org) in the hope of being able to help increase awareness and raise funds to assist the NGOs that work so hard to combat human trafficking and to support survivors of this terrible crime.

If you've got a story to tell, or just want to make contact with someone who might be able to understand how you feel, then please do write to me via the website. I would love to be able to include some 'survivors' stories' on it, so that other people can see that, however long and dark the tunnel may be, there can be light at the end of it.

Chapter 1

My brother's 18th birthday party was an elaborate event – a glamorous celebration that had been carefully planned by my mother down to the very last detail so that nothing could go wrong. We had a beautiful meal at a hotel with all our family and friends and when everyone had finished eating, my father took the microphone and announced that he'd been asked by my mother to give a speech about his eldest son. There were many good things that could be said about my brother, and a whole host of funny and touching anecdotes that could be told about him. So as the room fell quiet and everyone turned to look at my father, they were all smiling with a benign expectancy that quickly turned to horror when he announced that he could think of nothing to say other than that he was disappointed to have fathered such a 'useless piece of shit'.

For a moment, there was a stunned silence and then, as a low murmur of disapproval spread around the room, my grandfather leapt to his feet, snatched the microphone from my father's hand and, with tears in his eyes, began to talk about all the good things his grandson, Jason, had done and how much everyone in the family loved him.

When I eventually dared to look at my brother, he was sitting completely still, staring into the distance above everyone's heads with an expression of almost physical pain on his face. I looked away quickly, feeling sick, and wondered how any man could do such a terrible thing to *anyone*, let alone his own child, who was guilty of nothing other than trying for 18 years to gain his father's love and approval.

I think I knew in that moment that my parents' marriage was over, although it had a few more death throes to go through before they divorced.

Another event that finally tipped the balance for my mother occurred one night not long after Jason's birthday. I had come home from an evening out and, not realising that Jason and his girlfriend, Harriet, were babysitting for a neighbour, had locked the front door and gone to bed. Half an hour later, I was woken up by the sound of the doorbell. It rang just once, but almost immediately I heard footsteps thundering down the stairs and then Harriet's voice calling my mum's name and screaming, 'He's going to kill him. Help! Please! Someone *help!*'

My mother had already reached the top of the stairs by the time I'd jumped out of bed and rushed on to the land-ing. As I ran after her into the hallway, I could see Jason standing on the doorstep with blood pouring from his nose.

Harriet was sobbing and my father was waving his arms in the air and shouting, when suddenly Jason stepped forward, pushed Dad out of the way and yelled, 'You're a fucking wanker. I *hate* you. Why don't you go away and leave us all alone?' Then Jason rushed up the stairs and locked himself in his bedroom. My father smirked, shrugged his shoulders and went to bed.

Luckily, the commotion hadn't woken my younger sister and brothers, so Harriet, my mum and I went into the kitchen. For a few moments, we sat together around the table in a state of shocked disbelief, until Mum eventually broke the silence by asking the question that was in all of our minds when she said, 'What the hell just happened?'

It turned out that my father had been so annoyed at having been woken up by Jason's tentative ring on the doorbell that he'd flung open the front door and, without saying a word, head-butted his own son.

My mother sighed and lifted her hands off the table in a gesture of weary defeat as she said, 'Well, that's it then. I can't stand by and allow him to hit my children. That's one thing I'm *not* prepared to put up with.'

I felt terrible about what had happened – not just because I felt so sorry for Jason, but also because I knew it was my fault. Jason didn't have a key to the front door and

I hadn't made sure he was home before I locked it that night. Even now, I can't bear to think of the distress my thoughtlessness caused him.

So that was the second of the three 'final straws' for my mother. The last one came as a result of someone telling her that my father was seeing other women. When she confronted him, they'd been shouting and arguing for ages by the time I walked into the living room and heard Dad shout at Mum, 'She was a dead ringer for you, only *much* younger.' Then he stormed out of the room and Mum burst into tears.

It turned out that Mum's 'dead ringer' hadn't been the only woman Dad had been sleeping with. There were dozens of them. Apparently, he'd joined a group of swingers – not the sort who swap partners, but the ones who go to parties that have been organised for the specific purpose of having sex with total strangers, who are paid to do whatever weird and kinky things men like my dad want them to do.

When Mum left him, she discovered he'd remortgaged the house, not for financial reasons – he earned a considerable income and didn't have any money worries – but because he'd been siphoning money into foreign bank accounts. So Mum got very little money from the divorce, but she didn't really care, because all she wanted by then was to get away from my father and make a new home for herself and her children, where no one shouted at her and told her constantly that she was useless and stupid.

I was 17 when my parents separated, and I've rarely spoken to my father since then.

I was just a few hours old when I was placed in my father's arms for the first time. Apparently, I started to scream and he glanced down at me, handed me back to my mother and promptly lost all interest in me. It was an indifference that soon became mutual, and by the time I was in my early teens, I'd learned to accept the fact that I didn't like my own father. Fortunately, though, I've always loved my mum – as well as being a really good mother, she's my best friend and I can talk to her about almost anything.

I don't remember *ever* feeling any real affection for my father. He wasn't physically abusive when I was a child, but he *was* a bully, who only really communicated with his wife and children by shouting and swearing and telling us how useless we were. Gradually, over the years as I grew up, I almost got used to the way my heart started to thump whenever he was angry – which seemed to be most of the time. But I never got used to the things he'd do quite delib-erately to frighten us, or to his sick jokes, which often reduced me to tears of shock.

I was one of five children, all of us unplanned, unwanted by Dad and loved completely by Mum. My childhood was lived under the shadow cast by my father's verbal and emotional abuse, but it was Jason who suffered most as a result of his bullying.

Jason was a shy, cheerfully energetic child who hated the thought of doing anything wrong or of drawing people's attention to himself for any reason. Just imagining being late for school could reduce him to a state of hand-wringing anxiety, which our father always referred to as 'girly fussing' and which never failed to make him scornfully angry. In fact, Jason was about as far removed as it was possible for him to be from the kind of son our loud-mouthed, brashly over-confident father might have wanted – had he wanted a son at all.

It was heartbreaking to watch Jason trying so hard to please Dad, and although *I* learned from quite an early age to accept that none of us would ever be able to do anything right in his eyes, my poor brother never gave up hope of one day winning his affection. It was what Jason wanted more than anything else in the world, but it seemed that the more he tried, the more Dad intimidated and belittled him and the more nervous and, eventually, emotionally unstable Jason became.

Jason was the sort of child who always had everything organised for school the night before – his books in neat piles and his clean clothes laid out on a chair in his bedroom, so that all he had to do in the morning was get washed and dressed and he was ready to go. For me, however, the most important rituals of every morning revolved around making sure my uniform looked perfect and my hair was immaculate – which meant that I took rather longer to get ready than he did. And while

I was rushing around the house searching for my school bag or my books, Jason would stand by the front door, white with distress as he watched the minutes tick away on the grandfather clock in the hallway. Eventually, my father – who drove us to school most days on his way to work – would shout at him for looking so 'fucking pathetic' and then at me for being so disorganised and stupid.

I still feel sad and guilty whenever I think about all the times I made us late for school, although I didn't do it deliberately. We went to a good school and I think that, because I'd already accepted my father's opinion that I was 'inadequate', I was afraid of failing to meet the standard expected of us, to the point that making sure I was well turned out became almost an obsession. But I knew how much Jason dreaded the thought of having to walk into assembly on his own when everyone else was already sitting down, and I know it was my fault when, breathless with humiliation, that's exactly what he had to do on many occasions.

One morning, when Jason was 10 and I was nine, we were running late as usual and when I finally found my school bag, ran out of the house and jumped on to the back seat of the car beside my brother, Dad gave a self-satisfied smirk and said, in mock dismay, 'Oh dear, Jason, you're going to be late. Assembly will definitely have started by the time you get to school. You're going to have to walk in all on your own. Perhaps if you crawl on your stomach like a snake they won't notice you.' Then he threw back his head and laughed, amused by the image he'd conjured up and by Jason's clearly apparent anguish.

Jason began to cry and to plead, 'Please, *please*, Dad, try to get us there on time.'

But instead of making my father sympathetic – as you'd expect any man would be when his son was so blatantly upset – the sound of Jason crying seemed to act like a trigger that flipped a switch in his brain. He stopped laughing abruptly and as I glanced up nervously into the rear-view mirror, I saw his mouth twist into an expression of contempt and he suddenly shouted, 'You want to be early, do you? Is that why you're snivelling like a girl? Okay, Jason, we can be early.' Then he pressed his foot down hard on the accelerator, throwing us back into our seats as the car surged forward.

Sick with fear, I clutched so tightly at the seatbelt where it lay across my chest that my knuckles turned white and I could feel my fingernails digging painfully into the palms of my hands. For the next few minutes, we sped down one blurred street after another, while Jason hugged himself, rocked backwards and forwards, and whimpered.

I remember seeing a flash of colour ahead and catching a brief glimpse of the expressions on the faces of two men who were standing talking together at the side of the road. Beside each of the men was a bicycle, on which they were resting their hands casually and which toppled and fell to the ground as our car spun out of control and veered across the road towards them.

It was obvious that the men weren't going to have time to get out of the way. My father cursed and Jason and I screamed. By some miracle, we missed them by inches, my father managed to regain control of the car and we continued along the road at a slower speed while he shouted at us over his shoulder, '*See!* See what you've done, you little fuckers. You nearly made me kill those men.'

Jason was hysterical and I was sobbing, both because I was frightened and because I had a terrible sense of guilt. If we *had* killed the men – as it had seemed certain we were going to do – it would have been *my* fault because *I* had made us late. My father was right: I was 'fucking useless'.

When we arrived at school, Jason almost fell out of the car and then ran through the open wrought-iron gates, his shoulders hunched and his school bag clutched tightly to his chest as if he was trying to protect himself from physical attack. But I refused to follow him. Still shocked and shaking, I needed the comfort and reassurance that only my mother could give me. So I cried and screamed until my father took me home and then I sat in my bedroom, trying to block out the harsh, angry sound of my parents' voices as they shouted and argued with each other – because although my mother seemed to do little to deflect my father's nastiness when it was directed towards her, she somehow always found the strength to speak up in defence of her children.

The car incident was just one of the many, almost daily, occurrences during my childhood that made me realise my father didn't really like us. Someone once said that he simply didn't have the capacity to love anyone, and I think they were right. According to my grandmother, he used to delight in disappointing and upsetting my mother, even when they were first going out together. Apparently, no one had been able to understand why such a pretty, popular and cheerful girl agreed to marry such a sour, ill-mannered man. She did marry him, though, despite the fact that as the wedding car drove slowly along the streets towards the church, she knew she was making a terrible mistake. She once told me that although she'd loved my father, she would gladly have turned around at that moment and gone home again, still single, had it not been for the guilt she'd have felt about all the money her parents had spent and all their efforts to make it a wedding day to remember.

One morning a few months after they were married, when my mother was pregnant with Jason, my father rapped loudly on my grandparents' front door and announced to my bemused grandmother that her daughter was a 'soft piece of shit', of no use to man nor beast, and that he was returning her to her parents' tender care because he wanted nothing more to do with her. He took her back again, though – probably when he realised how inconvenient it was going to be for him to have to look after himself and the house. But this was a pattern he was to repeat many times over the next few years, and it wasn't long before my mother began to believe that she really was 'pointless', 'bloody irritating' and 'fucking stupid'.

Although my father often shouted and swore and constantly disparaged us all, he was rarely physically violent, and by the time I was in my teens I'd begun to answer him back. I think the fact that I was willing to stand up to him – verbally at least – made him back off a bit. But Jason – who, despite his almost permanent state of nervous apprehension, had a surprising amount of (groundless) optimism – kept trying to form a relationship with Dad and to win his approval. It was a hopeless task, however, and one that was to cause him nothing but heartache.

When I was seven, my mum gave birth to Emily and two years later to twin boys – the babies of the family, Mark and Jamie – all three of whom were 'accidents', just like Jason and I had been.

Although he hadn't had a stable or happy childhood or a good education, Dad was clever when it came to business and making money, so we lived in a very nice, big house in an affluent part of town. But I don't really remember him doing anything else specifically for any of us, and I often wondered why my mother stayed with him.

When she finally filed for divorce, protecting her children and escaping from my father's relentless denigration were Mum's main concerns. However, because money mattered so much to Dad, he couldn't believe she wanted nothing from him and he used to send her vicious text messages telling her he'd break her legs if she came after him for maintenance. He was angry with me as well – he always had been, for reasons I didn't understand – and one of the last things he said to me, with his characteristic turn of phrase, was, 'You're dead to me. You can rot in hell for all I care. I wouldn't piss on you if you were on fire.'

When our parents divorced, Jason continued to try to win Dad's approval and was so full of hurt and anger that he was spinning dangerously out of control. Until quite recently, I'd have said that my father didn't have any significant effect on my life – I told myself that as I didn't really like him, I could live with the fact that he didn't seem to love or care about me. I realise now, though, that being unloved by my own father not only made me feel unlovable, but also made me unsure about what loving someone really means, anxious about trusting anyone, particularly men, and afraid in case, like my father, I wasn't able to form loving, stable relationships. I had an image in my mind of living in The Little House on the Prairie, where everything was perfect and people were always kind to each other, and I decided that if I couldn't have *that*, I didn't want anything at all.

So perhaps it was surprising that I had *any* long-term relationships over the next few years. But I did – one with a man I loved and one with someone I thought I loved but who was really just a good friend. And then there was Kas, who, in time, became my *best* friend – not least, perhaps, because he was the opposite of my father in every way. Whereas Dad was loud, vulgar, self-engrossed and aggressively cruel, Kas was caring, charismatic and effortlessly polite. But even with Kas, who I first met when I was 18, it was a long time before I allowed myself to trust him. Once he did become my friend, however, he became quite an important part of my life and it felt as though he was the one person on whom I would always be able to depend.

Chapter 2

For a couple of years after my parents divorced, Jason was so angry about what had happened that he was in freefall. He still desperately wanted Dad to notice him and he turned against Mum, particularly later when she met Steve – the man who helped her return to being the person she used to be, who subsequently became our stepfather and who I wish had been my real father. Jason moved into a horrible, hostel-type flat miles away from where we'd grown up and, because he was determined to 'stand on my own two feet for once', he refused to let Mum help him in any way. Fortunately, though, he did eventually accept help from our grandmother and slowly started to sort himself out.

When I left school at 18, I was offered a really great job in Leeds. Dad had always been on at me about going to university, but I decided I wanted to stay near Mum and my young sister and brothers. So I took the job and moved into a flat in the city. I hadn't realised, though, how lonely living somewhere like that can be when you don't know many people, or how difficult I'd find it to move away from home and from the security and cocoon-like protection of my childhood. Apart from the friends I made at work, I didn't know anyone in Leeds, so I sometimes felt as though I was totally alone – until Serena got a job there too.

Serena and I had been friends at school and people always said we were like two peas in a pod. I loved having her close by again, and we soon became inseparable, going out shopping together and then having coffee at one of our favourite coffee shops while we examined the latest fashion magazines. My mother always dressed beautifully and as a child I'd loved watching her getting ready to go out. I wanted to look just like her, which is partly why I spent most of my earnings on good clothes and always paid special – almost obsessive – attention to my hair and make-up. The other reason, however, was that my father's constant criticism of me when I was growing up had left me feeling inadequate – not pretty enough, not clever enough, not good enough in *any* way – so I thought that at least if I was neat, tidy and 'well turned out', I'd know I'd done my best.

Every weekend, Serena and I went out to nice bars and a club – it soon became a routine that only sickness or a major

15

natural disaster would have made us deviate from. But I wasn't interested in meeting boys and having relationships – I had a deep distrust of men and was convinced that, on one level or another, they were all like my father. I just loved the dressing up, the dancing and the music, as well as the feeling that I was just like all the other young people who were out in the city centre having a good time. I was enjoying my life. But I suppose all good things have to come to an end, and when Serena took a job overseas for a couple of months, I more or less stopped going out at the weekends.

I'd been feeling increasingly unwell for quite a while and eventually I had to go into hospital for some tests to try to find out what was causing the severe stomach pains I kept getting. I'd made a good friend at work called John, and after Serena left we grew closer and he came to visit me in hospital. 'When they've found out what's wrong and you're better, we'll go away on holiday together,' he told me. 'I'll look after you. Just give me the chance to take care of you and make you happy.'

What he was offering me was what I'd always wanted and had only ever had from my mother: someone to take care of me and to care *about* me. John was three years older than me and he seemed to want to look after me, which I think is what I needed at the time. My parents' divorce had been miserable, and it was really nice to feel that, in the future, I'd have someone like John to rely on. He wasn't confrontational or threatening in any way and he took charge of my life and made me feel safe, so I allowed him to break through the protective barrier I'd built around myself and, before long, I moved into a flat with him.

I think I knew from the start that I didn't really love John, although I tried to convince myself I did, because I really wanted to. In reality, though, he was just a very good friend and someone I felt comfortable being with. For a while, everything seemed fine and then, gradually, he stopped wanting to do anything other than go to work, watch football on the television and go out with his mates, which meant I ended up sitting on my own, night after night, just waiting for him. I desperately wanted to be happy, but it seems that, sometimes, the more you want something, the more the opposite tends to happen. I wasn't even 20 years old and it was beginning to feel as though my life was slipping away. And then, just when it seemed as though things were about as miserable as they could be, Serena came back from working abroad and everything changed for the better.

One night, when Serena and I were in the club we always went to, she leaned towards me and, shouting to be heard above the loud, throbbing beat of the music, said, 'He's watching you.' She nodded her head almost imperceptibly in the direction of a group of uniformly dark-haired guys who were standing talking and laughing together at the side of the dance floor.

'Who? Who's watching me?' I shouted back. But I knew who she meant. I'd noticed him almost as soon as we started dancing.

The next time we went to the club, the same guy was there again with his friends, and as Serena and I danced, he kept trying to catch my eye. Whenever I looked in his direction, which I tried not to do, he smiled at me and I pretended I hadn't seen him. He was there the next time too, and the time after that, and then one night, when the music stopped for a moment and Serena turned to talk to someone she knew, I looked up to find him standing beside me.

'Will you ever talk to me?' he asked. The inflection in his voice – as well as his long-lashed, almost-black eyes – gave away the fact that he wasn't English, which I'd already pretty much guessed. I shook my head and said, 'No. No, I'm sorry. I don't want to talk to you. I don't want to talk to anyone.' Then the music started again and I moved away from him and began to dance.

Later, when I glanced towards the edge of the dance floor where he and his friends always stood, he was still watching me. This time, though, there was a hurt expression on his face that made me feel a bit guilty. And then I thought about my father and all the unhappiness falling in love had caused for my mother and I looked away without returning his rueful smile.

A few days after that, I was alone in the store where I worked when I heard the familiar scraping sound the door to the street always made as it was pushed open and I looked up to see him standing in front of me. I could feel the heat of a blush rising into my cheeks and I turned away from him quickly, hoping he hadn't seen the flash of recognition I knew must have been visible in my eyes. Then, muttering 'I'll get someone to help you', I scurried through the archway at the back of the store like a startled rabbit and hissed at one of the guys who was on his break, 'I have to go to the office. Can you speak to the customer who's just come in?'

I must have looked like an idiot and 'the customer' must have felt *so* embarrassed. But I'd been taken by surprise when I'd seen him standing there and, for some reason, my instinct had been to get away from him. I knew he hadn't opened the door by chance; there was absolutely no doubt in my mind that he'd come to see me. He came back two or three times after that and although I couldn't help but feel flattered by his interest and persistence, I did exactly the same thing each time.

Then, one evening, when Serena and I were at the club, the music stopped and he suddenly turned away from his friends, walked resolutely towards me, stood in front of me and said, 'I am Kastriot. My friends call me Kas. Would you like to go for a drink with me?'

I looked directly into his face for a moment and thought how kind his eyes were and how confident he seemed to be, particularly considering the fact that his previous attempts to talk to me had been so comprehensively rejected.

'No, thank you. I don't drink,' I answered, shifting my focus to a spot just above his left shoulder and praying silently that the conversation-stopping thud of music would start up again. But it seemed that God and the DJ weren't on my side.

'All right,' he said. 'Then we'll go for a coffee.'

'I don't drink coffee either,' I told him.

'Tea then,' he persisted. 'We will go together and drink tea. It is a well-known fact that everyone in England likes tea.'

I glanced towards him and saw that his smile had become tentative and the expression in his eyes had lost some of its confidence. Once again I felt mean, but I couldn't help myself from answering in a cold, unfriendly voice, '*I* don't.'

'Orange juice then?' He looked confused and I felt my cheeks blush with shame.

He spoke good English, with an accent that sounded Mediterranean, maybe Greek or Eastern European, and he was undeniably handsome. He was about my age I guessed, or perhaps a little older, and despite his clearly faltering self-assurance, he still had an air of quiet dignity, which was in sharp contrast to the brash resentment or feigned indifference I knew would have been the response of most of the boys I came across. He seemed genuinely bewildered by my refusal to engage with him in any way, and unafraid to show that he was hurt.

'I don't want to drink *anything* with you,' I told him, glaring at him fiercely. 'I do *not* want to go out with you. I have a boyfriend.' And, at that moment, God and the DJ relented and the room was filled with the thud of music, saving both of us from any further embarrassment. I flicked my hair to show my lack of interest and then turned away from him. Deep down, though, I knew I was acting like a stuck-up little snob and I hated being like that, but I *had* to protect myself.

Over the next few weeks, I got used to seeing him at the club every time Serena and I went there. It was our favourite club for many reasons – including the fact that we knew lots of other people who went there regularly and we always had a good time. And as he didn't make me feel uncomfortable or threatened in any way, it never crossed my mind to stop going there. In fact, I suppose I became a bit intrigued by him. It was difficult not to be flattered by his attention and by the way he never seemed to take his eyes off me, and the truth was that I liked the effect I had on him and maybe part of me wanted to see how long it would be before he gave up.

John and I were still living together, although we were leading increasingly separate lives and had become more like flatmates than boyfriend and girlfriend. What used to seem like being taken care of had begun to feel more like being treated as an incompetent child, but at least there was sometimes someone at home with me and I didn't always feel as though I was alone. I *was* on my own one evening, though, when my mobile phone rang and a number I didn't recognise came up on the screen. As soon as I heard his voice I knew that it was Kastriot, my persistent admirer.

'How did you get this number?' I asked.

'First, you have to ask "Who is this?"' he answered in a mock-serious tone.

'I know who you are,' I said. 'You're the guy who watches me at the club. I've told you, I don't want to talk to you. I'm not interested. Don't call me again.'

As I pressed the button to end the call, I felt uneasy. I knew we didn't have any friends in common, so how had he managed to get hold of my number? It seemed odd, but not enough to be any real cause for concern.

He phoned me a few more times after that, and each time I told him the same thing – that I didn't want to talk to him; I just wanted to be left alone. Then, one night at the club, when Serena and I were dancing and he was standing in his usual place at the side of the room, he caught my eye and started bowing down to me. It was ridiculous, but I couldn't help smiling and the next moment he was standing in front of me, pleading, 'Why will you never speak to me? I *have* to talk to you. Please don't make me suffer in this way. Let me take you away and marry you.'

I laughed as I said, 'You don't even know me!' But, despite the absurdity of what he was saying and the fact that I had no intention of responding to his interest in me, I felt a small thrill of pleasure. I was surprised, too, by how disappointed I felt when Serena and I went to the club one evening and he wasn't there; I told myself it served me right for being so unkind to him when all he'd been trying to do was talk to me.

He didn't come again after that and shortly afterwards Serena fell in love and we stopped going out together as often as we used to do. Each time I did go the club, though, I looked for him and, for reasons I didn't understand, felt a sense of missed opportunity when he wasn't there, as I was certain I would never see him again.

John and I stayed together for almost three years, although for a lot of that time we led separate lives and avoided acknowledging the fact that any romantic relationship we'd had was over. We were still together when I got a text message one day from a foreign number.

'Guess who?' it said, and I knew immediately who it was.

'It's Kastriot,' I texted back.

I don't know why I was so sure. I hadn't seen him for almost two years and there was no reason on earth for me to think of him then. But somehow I just knew.

Within seconds, I received another text: 'How can you know this? I noticed you but you never noticed me.'

So I described the leather jacket he used to wear, the way a thick, dark wave of his hair fell over his left eye and how he always stood at the side of the dance floor with his friends.

'So you *did* notice me!' he answered. 'Why were you always so mean to me? Why did you never talk to me? You broke my heart, but I've kept your number all this time.'

'I was horrible back then,' I told him. 'I hated all men and didn't want to talk to anyone. It wasn't just you. I'm sorry.'

I'd always felt guilty about the way I'd treated him. Although it had been obvious he liked me, he'd never pushed or harassed me or been unpleasant in any way, even when I'd been cold and unfriendly and had refused to give him a chance and get to know him.

'You were the most unapproachable girl I'd ever met,' Kas told me. 'It was as though you were in a bubble with a big sign on it saying *DO NOT COME NEAR ME*. You were the girl everyone wanted to talk to but no one dared to approach. You have no idea how much courage I needed to step forward and speak to you.'

'I'm ashamed,' I texted back. 'I didn't mean to be unkind to you. I was just trying to protect myself.'

'I fell in love with you the first time I saw you,' he answered.

I laughed as I tapped out the words, 'How is that possible? You can't love someone you've never really spoken to.'

'And you can't know how I feel,' he retorted. 'Every girl I see has your face. I can't get you out of my head. I remember everything about you – the song that was playing when I saw you for the first time, all the music you ever danced to, the clothes you wore, the way you smiled …'

I'd never met any man who talked about his feelings in that way and I didn't think for a moment that Kas was serious about loving me. And in any case, I was still living with John. But gradually, over the next couple of years – initially when he was living at home in Albania and later, when he moved to Italy – Kas and I became good friends. At first we just texted each other and then we began to talk on the phone, until eventually we were in almost daily contact and he had become the one person I could talk to about anything and everything that was going on in my life. When I was upset about something, he always seemed to understand and to say the right thing; when I was tired or fed up, he could make me laugh. And as my trust in him grew, I began to think that maybe I'd been wrong and not all men were like my father.

Even before I'd begun to talk to Kas on the phone, I'd been feeling increasingly stifled by my relationship with John. Ironically, his habit of taking charge and planning what we were going to do each day – the thing about him that used to make me feel so safe – was the thing that finally made me realise I wanted to get away from him. We seemed to have less and less to say to each other, and as I felt more detached from John, I grew closer to Kas. I would tell Kas about the arguments we were having and my suspicions that John was cheating on me, and he'd listen sympathetically and then say, 'I don't think this man is right for you. Maybe you shouldn't be with him.' And eventually, with Kas's help, I found the courage to leave and to tell John, 'I'm sorry. I don't love you and I can't do this anymore.'

John and I had been together for three years and even though our relationship had clearly run its course, splitting up was still hard. So I was grateful that Kas was always there, at the other end of a telephone, to help me through it. He was like a big brother as well as my best friend and he seemed to understand my doubts and suspicions. He made me feel as though I'd done the right thing in leaving John, and whenever I was miserable about it, he reminded me how good my life was going to be now that I was 'free'.

In reality, however, I was 21, had never really lived on my own, hadn't made many friends independently of John, and was frightened by the prospect of having to start my life all over again, alone. After Serena met her boyfriend, we'd more or less stopped going out together in the evenings. So I was grateful when Natasha, a friend I'd made at work, suggested a night out at a bar that had just opened. After that, she and I started going out together regularly and suddenly the future looked less bleak and lonely; life seemed to be full of possibilities.

And then, just a few months after John and I had split up, I fell in love.

Usually when I meet someone I'm attracted to, it's an instantaneous thing: I look at them and bang! – I'm smitten. And that was exactly what happened when I walked down the stairs at a nightclub with Natasha and the guy working behind the bar looked up at me with big, brown eyes. While Natasha bought us some drinks, I stood beside her with my back to the bar, trying to breathe normally and hoping that the sound of the music was muffling the heartbeat that I could hear thumping loudly in my head. Eventually, Natasha turned and handed me a glass and I said to her, 'That is the most beautiful boy I've ever seen in my life. I *have* to know who he is.'

It was quite early in the evening so the club wasn't yet heaving with people as it would be later and Natasha surveyed the dance floor with growing scepticism. Raising her eyebrows in mock bemusement, she pointed at a boy who was throwing his arms around like a demented wind-mill and asked: 'Who? *Him?*'

'*No,*' I hissed at her. 'Not there. The boy at the bar. The one who served you. *No.* Don't look round!' But it was too late, and as she turned her head to examine him, he looked up at her and smiled. Natasha smiled back at him sweetly and then scanned the room for a moment, pretending – unconvincingly – that she'd been looking at everyone. When she turned back to me she said, 'He's certainly good-looking,' laughing as she added, 'Oh I *see!* You're really serious.'

We'd planned to have just one or two drinks in that club before moving on to meet up with friends at another. But when the most beautiful boy in the world leaned across the bar and started talking to us, all I could think was, *I don't want to leave. Why did this have to happen tonight?* So, when Natasha touched my shoulder and I turned to see her tapping the face of her watch and nodding towards the stairs, my heart sank.

'Okay, well, we're going now. So … Well … Goodbye,' I told the barman, flushing crimson with embarrassment at the thought of how awkward and stupid I sounded.

'What do you mean, you're going?' he asked. 'You can't be leaving already.'

'Well, we have to meet some people and …'

And then I was walking up the stairs with Natasha, stepping into the cool night air and feeling as though I was about to burst into tears. *What if he's the man of my dreams,* I thought. *And I've just turned my back on him, walked away and let him go? What if I never see him again?* I started to feel as though I was going to have a panic attack, which was only averted by Natasha reminding me that, as he worked in the club, he would in all probability be there almost every night of every week.

When we returned the following Thursday, he saw us as soon as we walked down the stairs and by the time we'd reached the bar, he'd already poured two drinks. He handed them to us and said, 'You've come back!' and for a moment he looked directly into my eyes before turning to Natasha and smiling. But she just waved her hand, laughed and said, 'Oh, don't mind me. I'll just stand here and enjoy my cocktail!'

As soon as he spoke to me, my heart started to crash against my ribcage and my mind went completely blank. I tried to think of something to say, but all I eventually came up with was 'Hi'. Luckily, though, I said it at exactly the same moment as someone further down the bar caught his eye and, with an apologetic shrug, he moved away, while I turned to Natasha and cried, 'Oh my God! I can't even talk to him. What shall I do? I don't know what to say.'

'You'll be fine,' she told me, grinning as she lifted my hot, damp hand off her arm. 'Just take a deep breath and smile.'

And to my surprise it really was as easy as that. When he'd served the customer, he came back, and with our heads almost touching across the bar, we began to talk as though we'd known each other all our lives. Although his English was good, he spoke with an accent and when I asked him where he was from, he told me to guess.

'Albania,' I answered immediately and he almost dropped the glass he was holding.

'How can you possibly know that?' he asked. 'No one has ever guessed it before.'

From that moment, we became a couple. We went on our first date two days later and it was as though we had always been a part of each other's lives – me, the over-cautious ice queen who rarely spoke to men and didn't trust them when she did, and Erion, the kindest, gentlest, most beautiful man I'd ever seen. It sounds corny, I know, but it was as though he was the missing piece of a jigsaw I'd been searching for. John had filled the empty gap for a while, but had never really fitted the space like Erion did.

And it seemed that Erion felt the same. On our first night out together, he told me, 'I never notice anyone who comes into the club, but from the moment you walked in, all I could see in my mind were your eyes, just looking at me. I kept thinking, *What if she never comes back? What if I never see her again?* I couldn't bear the thought that I might have missed the opportunity to get to know the person I was meant to spend the rest of my life with.'

'I felt that too!' I told him. 'I felt as though I *had* to know who you were and that if I didn't find out, there would always be something missing from my life.'

Erion is still the only man I've ever truly loved, and I believe he's the only man who's ever loved me. One of the greatest regrets of my life will always be that I didn't fight with all my strength and determination not to lose him.

Chapter 3

After my first date with Erion, I couldn't wait to tell Kastriot all about him.

'I've met someone,' I blurted out when he next phoned me. 'I've been dying to tell you. And you'll never believe where he's from. Go on, guess.'

Kas sounded cool as he said, 'I don't know. Where is he from?' But I was too caught up in my own happiness and excitement to notice.

'He's from Albania!' I exclaimed.

'So?' Kas seemed almost angry. 'Why would you think that it would make me glad to know you're going out with someone and that he's from Albania?'

He had never spoken to me in such a sharp tone before and for a moment I was taken aback, and then disappointed by his coldness and lack of interest.

'But I thought you'd be pleased for me,' I said. 'I thought you'd be as amazed as I was that he's the same nationality as you are. How many people in England know *anyone* from Albania, let alone have a best friend *and* a boyfriend from there? Kastriot? Are you still there? I don't understand why you're not happy for me. You've always told me I can talk to you about anything and I thought you'd be happy because I'm happy.'

And then it struck me that maybe he was jealous. When he'd said he loved me in the text he'd sent me at the start of our friendship, I'd been certain he was joking – for humorous/dramatic effect – and I'd never taken it seriously at all. But now I felt my cheeks flush with embarrassment at the thought that perhaps there'd been at least a bit of truth in what he'd said.

It was an idea that was confirmed a moment later when he told me, 'I *do* want to see you happy, but not with another man. I do not want you to rub it in my face that someone else is taking you out and sleeping beside you in your bed.'

But for some reason I didn't seem able to absorb what Kas was telling me, perhaps because I didn't want to believe it was true. I didn't think about him like that at all; he was my best friend and I didn't want to accept that he might care about me in any other way because that would mean we'd lose the friendship we had. I was like a child, so focused on myself and on my own little world that I simply closed my mind to the fact that he might be hurt by my news. Because I was irritated with him for not reacting the way I'd wanted and expected him to, I didn't text him for the next few days. When he phoned me again and was his usual cheerful, supportive self, he was the first to mention Erion, and I felt an enormous sense of relief at the idea that, having thought about it, he'd realised our relationship was purely plutonic and that we were just good friends.

If I'd tried to imagine the man I'd fall in love with, I don't think I'd have come up with someone as wonderful as Erion. He was amazing, and when I look back on that time now, I can't believe I didn't recognise exactly what I had and that, instead of doing everything in my power to make him happy, I was sometimes unkind to him.

I know it sounds like a pathetic excuse to say I blame my father for the way I sometimes treated Erion, but in some respects I do. Every child wants – and has a right to expect – parents who love them, but when I was a child it seemed there was nothing I could do to make my father love *me*. So, eventually, I gave up trying. I told myself I'd accepted the fact that he didn't care about me and I stopped attempting to win his affection and approval. In reality, however, I never really came to terms with the way he let me down – and I still haven't, if I'm honest. It was more than just letting me down, though: he hurt me deeply, and then he abandoned us all and showed very clearly by his words and actions that he had never cared about any of us.

So, although I wasn't aware of it at the time, I think I was always testing Erion's love for me, stretching the bond that tied us together until it almost reached breaking point. Poor Erion must have wondered what on earth was the matter with me and why I kept pushing him away when it was clear to him – as it should have been clear to me – that what we had together was extraordinary. I was like a spoilt child, forever getting into huffs about things and telling Erion it was all over, although they never lasted longer than a day; then he'd come back and I'd cry and tell him I loved him and was sorry. I should have realised, though, that you can't keep stamping on something over and over again and expect it not to at least change its shape, even if it doesn't actually disintegrate into a thousand shattered pieces.

It was during one of our day-long break-ups that I started a new job, and when my co-workers asked if I had a boyfriend, I said, like Judas, 'No.' When Erion and I got back together again the next day, I would have felt stupid telling them I'd lied and that I did have a boyfriend after all. And, in any case, it didn't really come up in conversation again. So whenever Erion phoned me at work, I'd text him and tell him: 'I can't talk right now. I'll phone you later.' He must have known I was lying and he must have been really hurt and wondered why. But I couldn't help myself: there was something perverse and self-destructive in me that made it impossible for me to accept the fact that my life with Erion was happy and he loved me, although I know now that I wasn't as horrible to him as I blame myself for being and that, in reality, we were happy together most of the time.

Although we had our own flats, Erion spent most nights at mine – letting himself in with his key after he finished work at the club in the early hours of the morning – and I slept better knowing he was beside me. He cared about me and took care of me in the way that John had tried to do in the early days of our relationship but without doing the 'paternal disapproval' thing I'd learned to hate. And I am ashamed that I didn't always appreciate it at the time. For example, one morning, I had an appointment at the dentist and my mum picked me up just before 9 o'clock to drive me there. Erion had taken me to a previous appointment, but this one was early, when he'd normally be asleep after his night at the club, and Mum had offered to take me instead.

The dental practice was in a part of town I didn't know, and although I thought I'd remember the way from the last time I'd been, I didn't seem to recognise any of the streets when we got there. It was a rough area and as I directed us down the same street for the third time, some of the people standing at a bus stop turned to watch us and I could sense my mother's anxiety.

'How can you have forgotten the way?' she wailed, reaching out her right hand as she spoke and pressing the central door lock. 'This is a horrible area. We can't keep driving round and round in circles. We're already drawing attention to ourselves. For heaven's sake, Sophie, think! Which way do we go?'

'I don't know, Mum,' I answered. 'I'm sorry, but I just don't know where we are. I'll phone Erion.'

He answered the phone on the second ring, his voice husky with sleep.

'We're lost,' I told him tearfully. 'We've been driving up and down the same streets and I can't find the dentist.'

'It's okay, Sophie,' he said, immediately wide awake. 'Just tell me where you are.'

'I don't *know* where we are!' I cried. 'I don't recognise *anything*.'

'Well, tell me what you can see then,' he said. 'Just tell me what's in the street around you.'

So I described the large, square, red-brick Victorian building with its metal-shuttered windows and the litter-strewn patch of grass beside a small tarmac-covered play area on which stood a rusty swing and a battered seesaw. Erion made a small triumphant sound and said, 'I know where you are. Stay there and I'll be with you in 10 minutes.' And, just 10 minutes later, we saw his car driving down the road towards us.

'It's okay now,' he said, leaning in through my open window to kiss my cheek and then smiling at my mum. 'I will lead you. Follow me.'

'Thank you, dear,' my mother said, reaching across me to pat his hand. 'We're very grateful.'

But as soon as Erion had walked back to his car, I turned to my mother and said crossly, 'What *does* he look like? I can't believe what a mess he looks!' He was wearing his work trousers with a vest and no shirt, his hair was standing up on end like the comb of an agitated cockatoo and I think I was disappointed that my mum wouldn't see how perfect he really was – although nothing I tell myself now about why I said such a terrible thing makes me feel any better.

My mother was shocked and angry with me and told me, quite rightly, 'You should be ashamed of yourself. That boy worked till God knows what hour of the morning and then, as soon as you phoned him, he got up again and came out to help you. And all you can do is criticise the way he looks. Don't be so mean!'

Erion drove ahead of us to the dentist and then waited to lead us back on to the road that would take us home. To him, helping someone he loved and cared about was a normal thing to do – something instinctive he didn't even have to think about. But to me it was scary and unnerving because I wondered when he'd realise I wasn't worthy of that sort of love.

I was still talking regularly on the phone to Kas and whenever Erion and I had an argument, Kas would sympathise and advise me, and it really did feel as though I could tell him anything.

Sometimes, for no reason I could understand, I'd wake up in the morning, look at Erion lying asleep in the bed beside me and think, *I just want to be on my own.* Then, when he woke up and started to talk about what we could do together that day, I'd tell him I didn't want to spend the day with him and he'd look at me, his beautiful dark eyes full of hurt and incomprehension, and say, 'Why? Why do you do this to me?' And I never had an answer.

One day, when I got home from work and went into the bedroom to change my clothes, there was a piece of paper lying on my pillow. I hadn't been as nice as I should have been to Erion that morning, and as I picked it up with shaking hands and read the words that were written on it, I began to cry.

'To my beautiful baby,' it said. 'Every time I look into your eyes, I can see that you don't love me the same way I love you and I can't do this anymore.'

I closed my fingers tightly around the paper, crushing it in my hand, and then I sat down on the edge of the bed and cried. A few minutes later, as I slowly opened my hand again and tried to smooth the creases from the crumpled scrap of paper, I knew I had the answer to the question I was always asking without ever realising it: 'How far can I push the man I love before I push him away from me forever?'

I reached into the drawer beside the bed for a tissue and blew my nose. Then I wiped the back of my hand across my eyes, looked down at the paper again and read the last few words that were written on it: 'I can't be with you knowing you don't love me as much as I love you. I've tried, but it hurts too much and I know I can't do it anymore.'

I was sobbing as I pressed Erion's number on my phone, and as soon as I heard his voice I begged him, 'Please, Erion, I'm so sorry. Please don't do this. Of course I love you. Don't go. Please.'

It was what he'd needed to know, and before long he was holding me in his arms again. But, despite having had a glimpse of what my future might be like without him, I still couldn't always stop myself from testing him, and I'd sometimes ask, 'Do you really love me? You don't seem to notice me anymore and it sometimes feels as though you don't see me like you used to do.' And he'd answer, 'Of course I love you. I tell you this every day. How many times do I have to say it before you'll believe me?' But although he was patient and never spoke to me angrily or unkindly, I began to hear frustration in his voice.

My mother hadn't met Erion before that day when he came to guide us to the dentist, but as she got to know him, she became very fond of him. So, when I phoned her one day and told her I was unsure about our relationship and asked, 'What shall I do? I don't know if I love him. I don't know what I want,' she said, 'You can't keep pushing and pulling the poor boy. If you aren't certain you want to be with him, you have to tell him. It isn't fair to keep him hanging on if you don't really love him.'

I wished I could simply 'live in the moment', but when we'd been together for almost two years, I told Erion, 'I want to be on my own. I don't know if it's right for us to be together, so I think we should stop seeing each other.'

Finally, I'd stretched the bond between us so far that I'd found its breaking point and the sadness in his eyes almost broke my heart as he sighed and said, 'Okay, Sophie. I can't do this anymore either.'

This time, though, something seemed to have changed for me, and when he phoned the next day to say, 'Where are you? I need to talk to you,' my heart barely missed a beat the way it normally did.

'I don't want to see you,' I told him. 'I'm with some friends and I just want to go out tonight and have a good time. I'm sorry, Erion.'

Later, at a club in town, I was dancing with my friend Natasha, who was jigging around in front of me with her arms in the air, when I noticed her glance over my shoulder and look suddenly anxious. '*What?* What is it?' I asked her. But before I had time to turn around, two hands had covered my eyes and Erion said, 'Surprise!'

He dropped his hands on to my shoulders and spun me round so that I was facing him, and for a moment I wished I could return his smile, wrap my arms around him and tell him I'd made a mistake and was happy to see him. But, instead, I took a step away from him as I said, 'No, Erion. What are you doing here? I told you I didn't want to see you. You're just making this harder for both of us.'

He looked at me steadily for a moment, his eyes full of hurt and bewilderment, and then he turned abruptly on his heels and walked away.

For the next few days, he didn't try to contact me again and I told myself I didn't miss him and that it was for the best. And then, a couple of weeks later, I had a phone call from a girl called Lucy, who was the English girlfriend of Erion's best friend, Besmir. The four of us often spent time together, but I hadn't seen her since before Erion and I split up, and as soon as I heard her voice on the phone, I knew something bad had happened to him.

'He's in a holding cell at the airport,' she told me. 'He's going to be deported. He wants to talk to you.'

It felt as though something was being tightened around my stomach and I had to swallow several times to stop myself being sick. I knew Erion had come to England as an illegal immigrant 10 years previously, when he was just 14, but he'd recently applied for permission to stay. Although he still had family in Albania, he didn't want to go back there – not least because England had become his home and he'd made a good life for himself here.

'I don't understand,' I told Lucy. 'That can't be right. It doesn't make any sense. I went with him to the solicitor and she told him everything was going ahead and he'd been granted permission to remain here while all the paperwork was sorted out to make everything legal.'

Suddenly, it was as though I could see the future like a dark, empty tunnel ahead of me and I couldn't bear the thought of having to spend the rest of my life without Erion. Despite the way I'd sometimes behaved towards him, I think, deep down, I'd always believed he'd be there, waiting for me, if I ever needed him, and now it looked as though I might lose him forever.

'He's allowed to have one phone call,' Lucy told me. 'And he wants to talk to you. Please don't let him down, Sophie. He really loves you, you know.'

I was crying as I rang the number she gave me, and when he heard my voice, Erion cried too.

A couple of weeks previously, after we'd split up, he'd moved in to stay with an Albanian family who had already had their request to remain in England refused and were waiting to be told when they were going to be sent back to Albania. They hadn't realised that the immigration officers might simply turn up at their front door one day and they certainly hadn't expected it to happen so soon. Erion was out when the officers arrived, and when his friend phoned him to tell him what was happening and to say goodbye, he'd insisted on seeing the family one last time before they left the country.

Another friend who was with Erion when he received the call begged him not to go. But Erion told him, 'It'll be fine. I'm quite safe – I'm here legally at last. And I must say goodbye to them. They've been good to me, like my own family. I've got to go and see them.' And then he'd raced to the house, and had no reason not to give his name and details to the immigration officers when they asked for them. But, when they checked his status, they told him he had not been granted leave to stay and that he, too, would be deported back to Albania – a country he had not set foot in for 10 years, since he was a boy.

'I don't want you to worry about me,' Erion told me on the phone that day. 'I'll be all right. I have my family and …' He covered the phone with his hand, muffling the sound of a sob, and I cried as I told him I loved him and would never forgive myself for all the pain I'd caused him.

'I'll be fine,' he said again. 'I love you too, Sophie. And don't be sad – you haven't done anything wrong.'

But I knew I'd let him down – just as I used to let my brother down when I made him late for school – and I was devastated when, the next day, Erion's life was packed into a suitcase and he was deported.

When Lucy rang me again, she told me, 'Besmir and I have been talking, and if you really want to do something to help Erion, you could marry him.'

At first I didn't take the suggestion seriously, and then the more I thought about it, the more I realised Lucy and Besmir were probably right: if I married Erion, he'd be able to return to his life in England. But it was a decision that would affect my own life forever, and I still didn't know if I really loved him the way I wanted to love the man I married and who would become the father of my children. My mother had loved my father when she married him – although I'd never been able to understand why – and it had turned out to be a mistake that had caused her enormous unhappiness for many years. And that was part of the reason why I doubted my own feelings about Erion and why I wasn't sure whether what I felt for him was really love.

Eventually, I rang one of Erion's friends and told him what Lucy had suggested. He asked me to meet him for a coffee in town and later, when we were sitting opposite each other on leather armchairs in the coffee shop, Adnan sighed and said, 'Of course it would help Erion, and of course it would solve this huge problem for him, but you mustn't feel pressured into doing it if it isn't what you want to do.'

I *did* feel pressured though, for all sorts of reasons, and I still felt that way after I'd spoken to Erion on the phone and he'd insisted, 'Don't do this, Sophie. I don't want you to do it. It isn't the right thing for you and I don't want you to think I've only been with you for this reason.'

I laughed as I told him, 'I know you haven't. Don't be ridiculous.'

'But I don't want you to do it,' he persisted. 'Because then, if you regret it, you'll resent me. I'll find another way.'

But we both knew he wouldn't, and that marrying me was the *only* way.

Over the next few days, I felt as though I was being pulled physically from both sides. On one side were Erion's friends, most of whom were begging me to help bring him back to England and telling me, 'You've got to do this for him. He has no one else.' And on the other side was my mother, who, although she'd grown fond of Erion, was distraught at the idea of my going to Albania to marry him.

'How do you think I feel?' she said. 'How would any mother feel to see her daughter go off on her own to somewhere she knows nothing about? Please, Sophie. I don't want you to do this. I don't want you to go.'

I felt as though my head was spinning and although I tried to focus my mind on the pros and cons so that I could make a sensible decision, all I could think was, *Oh my God, what am I going to do?*

When my parents' marriage broke down, unhappiness spread like ripples in a pond to engulf us all, and I made a promise to myself then that I wouldn't ever get divorced. It was a promise I wanted to keep – for my own sake as well as for the sake of anyone who might get caught up in the misery – but I simply couldn't see any other way of helping Erion. One minute I'd be thinking, *I have to do this. I have to fly out to Albania, marry Erion and give him the chance to live his life here, where he really wants to be.* And the next I'd hear the little voice of caution in my head saying, *But what if it doesn't work out and you get divorced, and then you meet someone else and have to tell them, 'I've been married before, to a guy who needed a British passport'?* How would I ever be able to explain that to someone else, when even to me – who knew all the ins and outs of the situation – it sounded so awful?

While I was trying to decide what to do, I was still talking to Kas and he was vehement in his attempts to influence my decision.

'You can't do this,' he kept telling me. 'You don't have any idea what you'd be getting involved in. You're not thinking straight, Sophie. You don't love this man enough to make such a huge sacrifice for him.'

I understood the logic of what he was saying, but helping Erion seemed to be something I *had* to do – if not because I loved him enough to spend the rest of my life with him, then at least out of loyalty and because of what we'd had together for almost two years. I knew he was a good person and that, ultimately, I couldn't let him down and just walk away when he needed me. So I applied for a copy of my birth certificate, booked a flight to Albania and tried to close my mind to the fears and anxieties that kept crowding in on me. And I often wonder what would have happened if fate hadn't chosen that moment to step in and change the course of my life forever.

Chapter 4

I could hear the emotion in Erion's voice when I told him I'd made my decision. I don't think I quite managed to hide the fact that I was still anxious about what I was planning to do, but at least I no longer felt as though I was being buffeted on all sides by everyone's advice and opinions. I'd had stomach pains for a few days, which was gradually getting worse, and I was sure it was due to the stress I'd been under and that it would get better now that everything was settled. And then, four days before I was due to fly to Albania, I was rushed into hospital.

I'd woken up in the morning with a terrible pain and when I tried to get out of bed it felt as though a thousand knives were cutting into my stomach. I couldn't stand upright, and after stumbling to the bathroom, I rang my mother, who told me, 'Stay in bed till I get there. I'll be right over.'

When she arrived, she took one look at me and said, 'We're going to the hospital.' I began to argue, but she raised a hand to stop me and said firmly, 'This isn't a discussion, Sophie. Just do what I say.'

The young doctor who examined me had pallid, grey-white skin and a serious expression that did nothing to calm my anxiety. After he'd prodded and poked and asked me some questions, his voice was almost gloomy as he told me, 'We need to keep you in overnight.' Then, in a half-hearted attempt at reassurance, he gave a wan smile and added, 'Just so that we can do some tests to find out what the problem is.'

'Well, okay,' I said, glancing quickly at my mother, who nodded her head encouragingly. 'As long as it's just for tonight – I can't stay longer than that. I'm going away in a few days.'

The doctor shrugged – whether to signify agreement or an unwillingness to make any promises wasn't clear – and the next day I was examined again, scanned and slid into an MRI machine that made me feel sick and claustrophobic.

'It's likely that you've got a small twist in your intestine,' an older, more sympathetic doctor told me. 'Although it probably isn't too bad at the moment, it's a potentially dangerous condition if it isn't sorted out, so you need to have an operation as soon as possible.'

'How long will I have to be in hospital?' I asked him, rubbing the back of my hand across the hot tears that were rolling down my cheeks.

'About a week,' he answered. He looked at my mother, who was standing with her hands clasped tightly around the white metal rail at the foot of my bed, and smiled as he said, 'I'll leave you to talk things over. To be honest though, I don't think you really have any choice.' He turned, pushed aside the curtain that had been drawn around the bed and disappeared. Mum and I listened for a moment to the sound of his receding footsteps and then she sat down on the chair beside me and covered my hand with her own as I began to sob.

I had agonised for so long about going to Albania to marry Erion, and now that I'd finally made a decision, it seemed as though some unseen force was determined to snatch away the future I'd come to accept. My mother squeezed my hand, then she opened her handbag, handed me a tissue and stood up so that she could lean across the bed and hug me.

'Oh Mum,' I whispered into her shoulder. 'What am I going to do? I can't let Erion down. He's waiting for me.'

For a moment, she just stood there, hugging me silently. Then she sat down, took hold of my hand again and said, 'It's fate, Sophie. It's your angel looking over your shoulder. This has happened for a reason, and I'm certain it's a sign that you're not supposed to go. I've had a terrible feeling about it all along and now I'm convinced that it would have been the wrong thing for you to do. If you and Erion are meant to be together, there'll be some other way. But you weren't meant to go to Albania to marry him. I'm sure of that now.'

'I don't know,' I sighed. 'Maybe you're right.' I felt suddenly overwhelmed by tiredness and unable to think about anything anymore. Convincing myself that marrying Erion so that he would be able to return to live in England had involved so much heart-searching and so much mental effort that it was difficult simply to do a complete about-turn and believe the decision I'd made had been wrong. But I knew I had to have the operation – quite apart from anything else, my mother wouldn't have allowed me not to. So, the very next day, when I should have been packing my bags and getting ready to fly out to Albania, I was being wheeled into the operating theatre.

During the few days I was in hospital after the operation, I often lay in bed thinking, *I'd be boarding the plane now; now, I'd be with Erion; this morning I'd be getting ready to be married*. But there was nothing I could do about any of it, which, in some ways, was a kind of relief. Even today though, I sometimes wish I *had* caught that plane and married Erion, although, at the time, I don't think I fully understood exactly what it was I was intending to do. I'd just got swept up in it all, without ever imagining the reality of what would be involved. Perhaps I'd wanted to prove to myself that I wasn't like my father, that I *was* someone who could care deeply about other people and was prepared to risk everything for someone I loved.

As soon as I was able to leave the hospital, I went to stay with my nan and granddad, where I could recuperate in peace and quiet, and where my mother could visit me every day. I was in regular contact with Erion, too. He'd been desperately worried when I'd told him I'd been admitted to hospital for surgery, and every time he rang me he told me how frustrated and useless he felt because he couldn't be with me and take care of me when I needed him.

My mother, on the other hand, was trying to hide her relief. Although sympathetic to my confusion and disappointment, she was also determined to keep me cocooned and safe for as long as she possibly could, which is why, three weeks after I came out of hospital, Mum, Steve, Nan, Granddad, Emily, Mark, Jamie and I boarded a plane for a two-week holiday in Malta.

Only Jason couldn't come, because he was working, and at any other time, I would have loved being away with my family, but I couldn't relax. I felt sad because I'd let Erion down and guilty because I sometimes felt as though I'd been given a reprieve. He continued to phone me, to ask how I was and to tell me how much he missed me, but his calls made me feel even worse because I knew he felt the same as he'd always done, whereas I was afraid that the moment had passed and it was all over between us. He talked about the future and about the time when we would finally be together again, and as I listened to him, I felt as though my heart was going to break.

Eventually, I started to dread his calls and when my mother saw how unhappy I was and realised I was struggling to deal with the way I felt, she told me, 'You need to cut him off, Sophie. You can't go on hurting him like this, dragging things out so that he still has hope, when deep in your heart you know it's never really going to happen now. You have to tell him.'

I knew she was right, but I simply didn't have the courage to do it. So, instead, I took the coward's way out and stopped answering the phone when he rang. His voice-mails were heartbreaking. If there's some natural order in the world that requires people to be punished for being cowardly, those messages restored the balance in my case. As I sat listening to them, with tears streaming down my face, there was no mistaking the pain in Erion's voice as he pleaded with me to phone him, or even just to text him, so that he could understand what had happened and why I had decided I didn't love him anymore.

'I don't care that you didn't come,' he would say. 'I don't even care if you're never going to come. But I can't bear it if you don't talk to me. Please, Sophie, just pick up the phone and speak to me. I won't try to make you change your mind. You know I won't do that. But I love you and I just want to hear your voice.'

There were many, many times when I came close to snatching up the phone and telling Erion I was sorry and that I was going to book a seat on the next flight to Albania. Anything would have been better than having to listen to his bewildered unhappiness. But, somehow, something always stopped me from taking that step towards what I saw as an irrevocable commitment.

There were many times, too, when I sobbed to my mother, 'I can't do this. I simply *can't* hurt him like this.' And she would tell me, 'But you *are* going to hurt him, whatever happens. How can you be together? Do you not understand what that would involve? How can you make it work? You'd just be giving him false hope, which is far worse than no hope at all.' I knew she was right, so I cut him off without any explanation. I know I'll have to live with that guilt and with all the 'what-ifs' for the rest of my life.

The one light in all the darkness was that I still had my best friend to talk to. Kas had been phoning me regularly since I told him I'd had to have an operation and, as a consequence, wasn't going to go to Albania and marry Erion after all. He had been sympathetic and quick to assure me I'd made the right decision. And then, one day a few months later, he phoned me and said, 'I know how close you are to your mother, but I think you need a break from everything and everyone, even your family. You need to get away for a couple of days and forget about it all. I'm going to be in Spain next week, so why don't you come out and join me? Just have a weekend with no worries or stress.'

I knew that my mother – and all the other family members and friends who loved me – wanted what was best for me, but suddenly I realised just how much I needed to get away from my 'normal' life, even if only for just a few hours.

'I'll come,' I told Kas, and I was touched by how pleased he sounded as he said, quietly, 'That's great, Sophie. Book your flight and I'll pick you up at the airport.'

The two days I spent in Spain were better than I could possibly have imagined. It was like having been out at sea on a little boat during a terrible storm and then suddenly finding yourself safe and protected in the calm, still waters of a harbour. Kas made all the decisions and took care of everything, so that I didn't have to think at all. Although he was only a year or two older than me, I felt like a child in comparison. He was effortlessly charming, confident and in control; he knew exactly what he wanted in every situation and it seemed to me that there was nothing he wouldn't be able to do if he set his mind to it.

We had an amazing time together in Spain: we walked by the sea and skimmed stones across the waves, and then we sat on the beach and talked. And later, when we were standing on the promenade listening to a jazz band, Kas suddenly lifted me up into his arms and waltzed with me into the middle of the street while everyone around us laughed and applauded, their eyes misty with their own romantic memories. Then, at night, with our shoulders touching, we sat in perfect harmony, watching the stars and talking as though we'd known each other forever.

Kas told me about his studies, the languages he spoke and his plans and dreams for the future, while I thought how wonderful it must be to be as comfortable in your own skin as he clearly was. And, despite everything, I wondered what it would be like to live for the rest of my life with a man like that – who was the complete opposite of my father in almost every way, who knew where he was going and would sweep me along with him. Then, perhaps inevitably, I began to wonder if my mother had been right and it *had* been fate that had stepped in to prevent me going to Albania and marrying Erion. There was no doubt in my mind that I loved Erion, but perhaps Kas was the person I was supposed to be with.

Kas talked about how wonderful it would be if we could go travelling together and see the world. He described a life that wasn't all about going to work every day and being dragged down by the small things, but about really living, and as he drew me into the picture he was painting, I could almost believe that we could do anything together.

For every minute of every hour that I was with him, he was gentle, kind and considerate. I knew how he felt about me, so I was touched by the fact that he never pushed me to be more than just friends or made me feel uncomfortable. But although I still didn't have any romantic feelings towards him, by the time we said goodbye at the airport after the weekend, I couldn't help wondering what it would be like to be rescued by him from all the muddle and unhappiness that seemed to have engulfed my life.

He'd certainly been right when he told me that getting away from everything for a couple of days would do me good, and I returned home feeling, if not exactly optimistic about what lay ahead for me, at least that it might turn out not to be as difficult and as empty as I'd begun to think it would.

I felt as though the time had come to leave the security of living at home and go back to my job in Leeds. My flatmate had moved out and gone to work in London while I was away, and I hadn't anticipated how empty and lonely the flat would seem without her. The boost to my optimism and self-confidence that the weekend with Kas had given me didn't last very long once I was on my own, and I soon began to feel bewildered and mentally disorientated again. I'd come home from work every evening and a million questions would spin around in my head: *How did I end up here, lonely and miserable? Will I ever really be happy? What if every time I get the chance of happiness I mess it up? What if I simply don't have whatever it takes to be contented? How do people know when someone really loves them? How do you know that what you feel for someone really is love?* They were questions I could never answer and I began to feel as though I was losing my grip. So, when Kas phoned me a few weeks later and offered me the opportunity to break the cycle of craziness I seemed to be falling into, I was ready and willing to accept.

'I'm living in Italy now,' he told me, 'and I really miss you. Please come and see me again. There are so many wonderful places I want to take you to. Just come for a few days, for a holiday, and let me show you my life.'

It was the prospect of someone else taking charge and making all the decisions that was probably the most appealing aspect of the suggestion. I'd lost confidence in my own abilities and I felt as though I always got things wrong, whereas Kas seemed to know what to do in every situation. Although I'd had to take a lot of sick leave from my job, I still had some holiday owing to me, so I booked a week off work and flew out to Italy full of excited anticipation.

Kas was at the airport to meet me, as he'd promised he would be, and as he swept me up into his arms and squeezed all the air out of me, I thought how wrong I'd been not to have given him a chance four years earlier when he used to smile at me from the side of the dance floor at the club. I was 24 years old and I'd wasted a great deal of time pushing people away because I was unable – or unwilling – to trust anyone. But Erion had loved me and hadn't let me down. So perhaps it was time to consider the possibility that not all men were like my father and to trust Kas, too.

It was a decision that was to change everything, forever.

Chapter 5

We drove straight from the airport to a beautiful lake, where we sat together outside a café, soaking up the heat of the late-summer sunshine. Kas was exactly the same as he'd been in Spain – just as relaxed and easy to talk to – and I felt immediately comfortable in his company.

We went back to the lake that evening, and as the air was cool once the sun had gone down, we sat inside a restaurant, where we talked and laughed together and the waiter smiled at me and called me '*La bella signorina*'. Everything seemed perfect.

After the meal, we went to a café to meet two of Kas's friends, who were so nice to me I began to wonder what he'd told them about our relationship. At the café, we ate ice cream and drank brandy and when Kas and I were leaving, the two men stood up, kissed me on both cheeks like benevolent uncles and said '*Arrivederci, Soffee*'.

That night, in Kas's apartment in an ancient, yellow-brick house a couple of miles from the centre of town, we made love for the first time, and afterwards Kas held me in his arms and I felt safe. I didn't know whether I was falling in love with him; I certainly didn't feel the way I used to do when I was with Erion, when a light seemed to shine from somewhere deep inside me, but maybe I'd been wrong and that hadn't been love, whereas the feeling of security I had with Kas was.

For the rest of the weekend, we wandered around the city together, sat outside cafés drinking coffee or glasses of wine and ate our meals in restaurants that were full of the sound of laughter and where everyone seemed to talk at the same time. On the Saturday evening, we went to an elegant nightclub in the centre of town, which was decorated with lavish crystal chandeliers and carved-marble fountains and was quite unlike any nightclub I'd ever been to before. Home, with all its worries, seemed a million miles away.

We spent Sunday by the lake and when we returned to Kas's flat in the early evening, I had an almost physical sense of contentment. Kas's arm was resting lightly on my shoulders as he put his key in the lock of the front door, and I reached up to kiss his cheek before walking across the little hallway and into the bathroom.

When I came out again a few minutes later, Kas was in the kitchen. He had his back to the open doorway, but he turned as I stepped through it and looked at me with an expression I didn't recognise and couldn't read. Although he didn't seem to be angry, there was a coldness in his eyes that made the skin on my scalp tingle and my heart began to race.

'Is everything all right?' I asked him. 'Kas? Is something wrong?' But instead of smiling and reassuring me, as I'd hoped he would do, he nodded his head towards the little wooden table under the window and said, in a voice that filled me with dread, 'We need to talk.'

I pulled out a chair and sat down, expecting him to sit beside me, but he remained standing, with his back resting against the work surface, as he said, 'There is a reason you are here.' I looked up at him and smiled, but when he didn't smile back at me, I felt my stomach contract sharply.

'There is a reason,' he said again, 'and I am going to tell you what it is. First though, I have to ask you: do you love me?'

'I think I do,' I told him, trying to ignore the horrible sense of foreboding that had settled over me like a dark shadow. 'I don't know how people know when they love someone, but you've been there for me for so long that ...'

He interrupted me, raising a hand impatiently and saying, 'Well, if you love someone, you have to make sacrifices for them. We all have to make sacrifices for the people we love, and that's why I asked you to come here: because there's something you can do for me. There's a sacrifice you can make to show me that you love me.'

He didn't raise his voice at all, but I could feel his irritation and when he looked at me, his expression seemed to be almost one of disgust. He spoke slowly, as though explaining a very simple concept to a determinedly slow-witted child, and although I nodded to indicate that I understood what he was saying, I didn't actually understand it at all.

When he spoke again, he sounded angry, in a way I'd never heard him sound before, and he barely glanced at me as he said, 'As you say, I have always been there for you and now you must repay me by doing something for me.'

'Okay,' I told him. 'You know I'd do anything I can to help you. But, please Kas, don't look so serious. You're making me nervous.' And then I laughed, because I knew I didn't have to be afraid. This was Kas, who never shouted, who had been my best friend for the last four years and who I knew was the one man I could trust, apart from Erion.

'I've got a debt that has to be paid,' Kas said. 'That's why you are here. You are going to repay this debt for me.'

His eyes had become cold and there was a closed, hard expression on his face. But still I told myself there was nothing to be afraid of. After all, what possible reason could Kas have for being angry with me?

'Of course I'd help you if I could,' I told him. 'But I hope I haven't given you the impression that I've got money. I spend almost everything I earn, so I don't even have any savings. I don't know what …'

Again, he interrupted me and I could almost feel his irritation as he snapped, 'This is what you're here for. You are here to help me to repay this debt. This is why I asked you to come to Italy. It's a sacrifice anyone would be happy to make for someone they loved.'

I felt sick. I couldn't understand what Kas was really saying or why he'd suddenly become so coldly detached. My heart was pounding and tears had begun to spill over on to my cheeks. I wanted to say to him, 'This isn't the way we are together. Why are you speaking to me like this?' But he was watching me with an expression so close to dislike that the words stayed locked inside my head.

'I'm in trouble,' he said. 'I owe a hundred thousand Euros – to Mario in fact, one of the men you met at the bar after dinner the other night and found so charming. I have to pay this debt.'

'Oh Kas, I'm so sorry!' I cried, although if I'm being honest, I'd have to admit that my sympathy was mingled with relief at the realisation that he wasn't angry with me after all. When he'd first mentioned a debt, I'd assumed he meant it figuratively, as he wasn't at all the sort of person I'd have imagined getting into financial debt. He'd never talked in any detail about his work – only ever referring to it as 'the import and export business' – but he seemed to have a comfortable life and I suppose, if I'd thought about it at all, I'd have assumed he earned a fairly good income. But I knew enough about him to know how much he must have hated having to ask for help, so I tried not to sound surprised or pitying as I asked, 'What happened?'

I don't know what I expected him to say – perhaps that someone in his family had been ill and had needed expensive medical treatment and that he'd had to send home more money than he had. So I was caught completely off guard when he said, 'It was a drugs' deal that went wrong.'

At first I thought he was joking – giving me a ludicrously unlikely explanation in an attempt to make light of a situation that embarrassed him – but his face remained completely serious as he continued, 'If I don't pay the money back, it will cause problems for my family. So that's why I need you to make this sacrifice for love.' And that's when my heart began to race and the palms of my hands became damp with sweat.

For a few seconds, I just looked at him, my mind totally blank and uncomprehending, and then I shrugged and said, 'I don't know what you mean. How can *I* help you? You know I want to, but it would take me a lifetime to earn that sort of money.'

'I don't expect you to earn it in your pathetic job in England.' His sneer was cold and dismissive. 'You will earn it here. I will find you a place to work – on the streets.'

Again a wave of relief washed over me and I laughed as I said, 'Don't be ridiculous! Work on the streets doing what?' And then I added hastily, 'But don't worry, Kas. I *will* help you. We'll think of something, I promise.'

'*We* don't need to think of anything,' he snapped, and the unmistakable sound of anger and dislike in his voice filled me with dread. '*I have already thought of something, and that is why you are here.*'

He took a step towards me and, instinctively, I cowered away from him.

'What's your problem?' he shouted, leaning down so that his face was just a couple of inches away from mine. 'Why are you looking at me like that? How dare you disrespect me in this way?'

It was as though the temper he'd only just been managing to control had finally erupted, and his face was contorted unrecognisably as he demanded, 'How dare you answer me back? Do you not know that if you love someone, you have to make sacrifices for them? Are you so selfish that you can't do this thing for me?'

I felt like an actor who'd walked on to the stage to speak my lines and realised I'd learned the wrong part in the wrong play, so that everything going on around me was completely incomprehensible. And then it suddenly struck me, almost like a physical blow, that the 'work on the streets' he was talking about was prostitution.

A wave of nausea washed over me, followed swiftly by embarrassment at the thought that I must have misunderstood. *He doesn't mean it*, I told myself. *Just keep calm. This sort of thing doesn't happen in real life.* But Kas was clearly in deadly earnest and as I rested my elbows on the kitchen table, holding my head in my hands with tears streaming down my face, I was afraid. The last man I'd ever been afraid of was my father, and as I looked at Kas, all the old feelings of dread and helpless vulnerability that I'd been so determined never to experience again threatened to overwhelm me once more.

Kas strode backwards and forwards in front of me, sometimes shouting, sometimes speaking in a quiet voice that was even more menacing and frightening than his anger. Then, suddenly, he leaned down towards me again and screamed, 'Who do you think you are, woman? Do you think that after I've waited for you all these years I'm just going to let you go? Well, you're wrong. I'm not letting you go. Do you understand? I will *never* let you go. You are mine now. Your life belongs to me, and you will never get away from me.'

And that's when the thought struck me that perhaps he was actually crazy. No one who was sane could possibly say the things he was saying: men like Kas aren't pimps – or drug dealers – and girls like me don't work on the streets. The idea was absurd and, in any case, how could anyone actually make someone else do that? But, whether he was crazy or not, the fact remained that Kas was in a rage – apparently with me, although I didn't understand why – and I was very frightened.

I kept telling myself he'd be all right again in the morning. We just had to get through the night and he'd have got over whatever had upset him. And if he hadn't, I'd simply tell him, 'I'm not going to do it. I thought you knew me. If you did, you'd know I would never do that in a million years. I'm sorry about the money you owe, but I can't help you in that way.' Then I'd make some excuse to cut short my visit and go home – to the 'pathetic' job I enjoyed, the family I loved and my 'normal' life.

I wrapped my arms across my chest and hugged myself tightly, trying to control the violent shaking of my body, and Kas pulled out a chair and sat down opposite me at the table. *Thank God*, I thought. *He's calming down at last. Now he'll tell me what's wrong and that he's sorry. Whatever I do, I mustn't antagonise him. Just think, Sophie. Think before you speak.*

He began to talk in a quieter voice, telling me what had happened as though he was discussing an ordinary, every-day event. But I'd never taken drugs and I didn't think I knew anyone who had, so to me it sounded as though he was describing a scene from a film.

'I was smuggling cocaine to Holland,' he said. 'And when I realised the police were following me, I threw it out of the car. Now the dealer wants the money he lost.' He shrugged. 'That's just the way it goes. The coke's gone and Mario wants his cash. That's why he wanted to see you the other day – to make sure you'd be able to earn the money for me.'

'*What*? Oh my God!' I stared at him, anxious for a moment that I was going to be sick, and then I pressed my forehead on to the cool surface of the table and tried to process the disconnected jumble of my thoughts.

'So, as you can see, I have no alternative.' Kas leaned back in his chair, stretched his arms in the air above his head and yawned. 'There's no other way for me to raise the money. I could use other girls, but I wouldn't be able to trust them the way I know I can trust you. I know you'll be loyal to me and that you would never do anything to disrespect me.'

'We can work something out,' I told him, lifting my head from the table and wiping my face with the back of my hand. 'I'm sure that if we think about this together, we can …'

'I know you won't disrespect me,' he said, looking past me and out of the window. 'Because if you did, if you even thought about it, I would find out and there would be consequences.'

I knew people didn't say things like that in real life, but however much I tried to tell myself it was all some elaborately cruel joke, I knew in my heart that he meant every word and that I'd made a huge and potentially fatal error when I'd allowed myself to break my golden rule and trust him. Already emotionally exhausted and bewildered, I was suddenly overwhelmed by the need to be at home, where my mother would put her arms around me and tell me 'It'll be all right, love'. Instead, though, I was alone in a foreign country with a man who professed to love me but who was asking me to do something no one in their right mind would ever ask anyone to do.

I began to plead with him: 'Please. *Please* don't make me do this! There must be some other way for you to repay the money. I can't do what you're suggesting. Please, Kas.' I was still pleading with him when, without any warning, he reached out his hand and grabbed me by the hair, forcing my head backwards so that I was looking up into his face as he shouted, 'It isn't a suggestion, woman. How stupid are you? Don't you understand? You've grown up in a world full of *nice* things, where you've never had to face the cold reality of many people's lives.' He sneered as he said the word 'nice', twisting his fingers in my hair so that it felt as though a million needles were digging into my scalp. 'You have always lived in a world where the only thing you have to cry about is the fact that "Daddy doesn't love me".' He mimicked the voice of a whining, spoilt child, and then his tone was cold again as he said, 'You think that means you've had a hard life? You have no idea what a hard life is. You have no idea about the things some people have to do because, in their lives, there *is* no other way.'

'I *don't* think that,' I sobbed, a small spark of indignation burning inside me for a moment.

In all the time I'd known Kas – or *thought* I'd known him – I'd never seen the slightest indication that he could be violent, and somehow it was the abrupt and very emphatic change in his behaviour and his attitude towards me that made me most afraid of him. My mind simply couldn't process or make any sense of all the new information it was being presented with. I kept thinking that if only we could talk things through logically, we'd be able to come up with a more realistic solution to Kas's financial problems.

I was so confused that I wasn't certain about anything anymore, except, perhaps, that Kas wasn't really intending to make me do the things he was talking about. So, even if I hadn't been as frightened of him as I had instantly become, I don't think I'd have tried to run away and escape from him. All I needed, I told myself, was to find something to focus on that would anchor me once again to the real world I was used to and could understand.

I'd never even heard Kas swear before that day, so although I was shocked by the things he was saying, I was completely unprepared for what he said next. His tone was contemptuous when he asked me, 'Do you think you're the only woman who's ever worked on the streets for me?' Then his mood seemed to change and he stretched out a hand to touch the top of my bowed head almost affection- ately before saying, 'But you're different. The other girls were all bitches. Do you know what a real whore is?' Suddenly, he grasped my hair again, yanking my head back and upwards so that I was forced to look at him, and shouted, 'Well, do you?'

I closed my eyes and tried to shake my head.

'A whore is a woman who treats a man with disrespect by cheating on him when she's going out with him. That's a *real* whore!' He sounded almost triumphant, and he smiled as he added, 'But a woman who sells herself to make money is just being clever. Your pussy will be a goldmine.'

I began to sob, lifting my feet onto the chair in front of me and clutching my knees to my chest to try to stop my body shaking, and Kas exploded into uncontrolled rage. 'If you give me that look again,' he screamed, 'if you disrespect me one more time, you'll see what I will do! How *dare* you? How dare you do this to me?' I dug my fingernails into my thighs and told myself, *Stop, Sophie! You have to stop crying. Don't let him see your fear. Your tears are making him angrier.* And, as if he'd read my thoughts, he bellowed at me, 'Stop it! How *dare* you cry? How dare you do this to me? Just look at yourself! You look terrible. Go to the bathroom and straighten your hair. Pull yourself together, woman, for God's sake. Go! Go to the bathroom and see how bad you look.'

Still sobbing, I stood up, edged around the table and scuttled out of the kitchen, with the sound of Kas's fury echoing after me as he called, 'Don't close the bathroom door. Leave it open.' And already I wouldn't even have dreamed of disobeying him.

In the bathroom, I looked in the mirror at my white, tear-stained face and the wild untidiness of my hair and it was as though I was looking at a stranger. I knew something profoundly significant had just happened, but as it didn't fit anywhere on my own spectrum of reality, I couldn't make any sense of it. And then I began to panic as the thought struck me that if I stayed in the bathroom too long, Kas might be angry with me.

I quickly tugged a brush through my hair, splashed water on to my face and crept back into the kitchen, where he was leaning against the sink. His voice was almost tender as he asked me, 'You love your little brothers, don't you?'

'Yes, yes, I do,' I answered hastily, relieved to talk about something normal and praying that the thought of how much I would miss my family might make him decide to let me go home.

'How old are the twins? Thirteen? Fourteen?'

'They're thirteen,' I said, trying to speak in what I hoped was a 'respectful' tone of voice.

'Hmm.' He smiled at me and I felt an almost imperceptible glimmer of hope, which was shattered instantly when he said, 'So you would be very sad if anything happened to them?'

It sounded like a question, although I knew without any doubt that it was a statement – or, more precisely, a threat.

'Of course, I know where your family lives,' Kas continued, twisting his body slightly to one side so that he could pick up a carving knife, which he turned slowly in his hand. 'So, if you disrespect me again, I will have your precious little brothers taken from their home. It will happen as easily as that.' He stepped forward and clicked his fingers in my face. 'You have no idea what I can do. If you ever try to get away or do anything to disrespect me, I will have your little brothers taken, just like that.'

He snapped his fingers again and as the sound rang out like a shot from a gun, the room began to turn and I sank to my knees on the floor, screaming silently in my head,

No! Oh my God, no! This can't be happening. It isn't real. What am I going to do?

Kas pulled me up roughly by my arm and pushed me towards the open door. I could sense his disgust as he spat out the words, 'Get out of my sight! Go on! *Go!* Go to bed, and tomorrow I'll take you to see where you'll be working.'

That night I slept in a single bed in Kas's bedroom, although, in fact, I barely slept at all. My mind was racing, and every time I began to slip into exhausted oblivion, my eyes snapped open and I'd try again to concentrate on thinking of some excuse that would convince Kas I had to go home. I attempted – without success – to comfort myself with the thought that, *Tomorrow everything will be okay. When he wakes up, he'll be all right again. I'll explain to him that I don't want to do it and he'll understand. Everything will be fine.*

In the morning I told him, 'I've got to go home. I can't just leave my family and my job. And I can't do what you're asking me to do. I don't want to do it, but even if I did, I can't because of the operation and the problems I've had …'

He'd shrugged his shoulders and made a dismissive 'pfff' sound when I'd mentioned my family, but suddenly he erupted into fury and shouted, 'Don't be so ridiculous, woman. You're being a hypochondriac. You've had your operation. It's over. There's nothing medically wrong with you. You're fine. You need to stop thinking about yourself and your imagined illnesses and think about all the people who are far worse off than you are.'

But on that first morning of the new life Kas had planned for me, all I could think about was finding some way to explain to him why I couldn't stay in Italy and work to pay off his debt. I told him all the excuses that had sounded so reasonable in my head during the night, but he didn't even listen. For four years, he'd been nice to me. Even when I'd told him on the phone that I'd met Erion and he was upset and said he didn't want to hear about my new boyfriend, he hadn't sounded angry. And then he'd said he was in love with me. So I still couldn't believe that when he realised how distressed I really was, he wouldn't change his mind and tell me he was sorry and of course I didn't have to do the horrible things he'd talked about. What I hadn't yet understood, however, was that Kas's idea of what was normal and acceptable was quite different from the normality of most other people.

'Please don't make me do this,' I begged him again. 'I want to help you, but I really can't do what you're asking.' And again he shouted, 'Don't you dare to disrespect me,' slapping me so hard across the face that he sent me flying into a corner of the kitchen, where I cowered on the floor. 'You will do whatever I tell you to do,' he bellowed. 'If you try to make contact with *anyone* without my permission, your family will suffer. Is that you want, woman? Are you so selfish that you'd let something bad happen to your precious little brothers just because you have to do something you don't want to do?'

I shook my head mutely.

'Do you think anyone will listen to you anyway?' He took a step towards me as he spoke and I recoiled, covering my head with my hands and pressing my body against the wall. 'Do you think anyone will care what happens to you? All you are now is a piece of pussy on the street.'

The harsh crudeness of his words made me flinch and he laughed as he asked, 'Do you know what Italians like most?' It didn't seem to be a question that required an answer, but he suddenly bent down towards me and shouted, '*Do* you?'

'No, I don't know,' I whispered.

'The three Ps,' he said, smiling his humourless smile. 'Pussy, pizza and pasta. So who's going to give a fuck about what happens to you?'

Chapter 6

Kas's flat was in a residential area on a hill just outside town and as we drove down the winding street to the main road, he kept up a constant stream of criticism and harassment, while I stared blindly out of the window. A few hundred metres along the road that ran into town, he turned the car onto a dirt track that led around the back of a petrol station, nodded his head towards a small wooded area beside a solitary house and said, 'This is where you'll be working.'

I looked in the direction he indicated, half-expecting to see … something, I don't know what. But there was nothing, just a small, dark copse of trees – which looked gloomy even in the bright morning sunshine – and the dusty, unlit track.

'This is where you'll come with your customers,' Kas told me. 'It must be *this* spot, nowhere else. It's the only place you can't be seen from the house.'

Tears began to trickle down my cheeks and as I pressed my forehead against the window, I thought, *Why is he telling me this? Why is he carrying on pretending that this is going to happen? None of this is real.* But when he drove back onto the main road and said, 'This is where you'll wait to pick up your customers,' I began to realise that, in his mind at least, it *was* a reality.

He drove on along the road, slowing down as we passed a patch of dry grass and saying, 'This is another place you can wait.' There was no pavement and almost no streetlights, and I couldn't imagine what it would be like to stand there alone at night. My head was spinning as I tried to take in the long list of instructions he was giving me. Then he said, 'When someone stops, he'll ask you how much,' and he taught me the numbers and Italian phrases I'd need to know, testing me and making me repeat them until he was satisfied I'd be understood.

'When you've given him the price,' Kas told me. 'He'll either say "Get in" or he'll drive off. If you get in, you ask "*Bocca* or *fica*?" – it means "Mouth or pussy?"'

Just hearing the words made me feel sick with disgust, and I knew I couldn't possibly say them – let alone *do* with a stranger the repulsive things Kas was talking about.

As we drove down the road from his flat earlier that morning, I'd tried to memorise some landmarks, so that

I'd be able to get my bearings if I ever managed to escape. Now, though, I knew with absolute conviction that that was never going to happen. Kas had told me the night before, and again several times during the day, that if I tried to get away, he'd find me. He'd already hit me and pulled my hair so hard that great clumps of it had come away in his hand, and when he described how he'd 'passed on' to someone else a girl who'd proved to be 'thick and stupid', and told me he wouldn't hesitate to do the same to me if I disobeyed or disrespected him, I had no reason not to believe him.

In my 'real' life, I'd simply have said 'No, I won't do it', and walked away from him. But I already seemed to have lost any ability I'd ever had to stand up for myself. The previous evening, Kas had snatched up my bag, taken out my mobile phone, passport and purse, which contained all my money and my credit card, and slipped them into his pocket. In doing so, he seemed to have taken control of my life, and I was completely powerless to do anything about it. I felt as though I was tumbling through space, unable to save myself and dreading the inevitable moment when I hit the ground.

It was hard to believe that in just 24 hours I'd learned to be frightened of the man I'd thought was my best friend. I felt confused and disorientated, although in my mind there was still just one certainty: that he would stop at nothing to safeguard himself and get what he wanted, which meant that he wouldn't hesitate to carry out his threat to harm my little brothers if I defied or disobeyed him in any way.

As we drove along the main road, Kas continued to give me instructions – although sometimes he could have been speaking a foreign language for all the sense I could make of what he was saying. Suddenly, my heart began to race as I realised he'd asked me a question. 'Are you listening to me?' he shouted. 'Look at me, woman, when I'm talking to you.' Before I had a chance to turn towards him, he reached across the car and hit the side of my head, smashing it against the window and sending a sharp pain shooting down through my neck and into my hunched shoulders.

Although I was shocked and taken by surprise, I didn't make a sound, and Kas just continued talking as though nothing had happened. 'You must always have two packets of tissues, a packet of baby wipes and plenty of condoms,' he said. 'You *never* do it without using a condom and never, *ever*, anally.' He looked disgusted as he added, 'That would be wrong.'

Wrong? Was that really the only part of it that he thought was wrong? I felt as though I was trapped in some surreal nightmare.

'The price you give them is for 15 minutes – maximum,' he continued. 'If they take longer, the cost is more. You never agree to go with someone to a house without telling me first. If you call or text me, you must immediately delete that call or text from your phone log. Do you understand?'

'Yes,' I whispered. 'But I'm frightened. What if someone hurts me? Please Kas, don't make me do this. There must be some other way.'

'Who's going to hurt you?' he snapped, lifting his hands off the steering wheel so that I cringed back against the window, anticipating the next blow. This time, though, instead of hitting me, he patted my knee and laughed as he said, 'You're not important enough for anyone to bother to harm you.' Then his mood changed abruptly again and, in a tone that was cold and threatening, he added, 'If anything ever happens to me, if I'm traced because of your stupidity or because you haven't done exactly what I've told you to do, you will be punished. If you cheat on me or try to hide money from me or break the rules in any way, believe me, woman, you will be sorry. Do you understand?'

And again I closed my eyes, nodded my head and whispered 'Yes'.

'You go only with Italian men,' he told me. 'No blacks, no Moroccans, Moldovans, Albanians, Romanians …' The list was long and I began to panic as I listened to his descriptions of all the characteristics and mannerisms that, apparently, would enable me to distinguish one race from another.

'But what do I say?' I asked him. 'How do I explain to them that I can't go with them?' The very thought of having to reject someone because of their race made me feel sick with shame and anxiety. But Kas just looked at me with an expression of exaggerated bewilderment and said, 'You say no.'

And what if they ignore 'No', like you've done? I thought, although already I knew I would never dare say such a thing to Kas out loud.

A sick feeling of dread settled like a weight in my stomach as he taught me how to say in Italian 'No blacks', 'No Albanians' and 'No' to all the other nationalities I had to refuse. And then he told me, 'The Eastern Europeans and the Moroccans – especially the Moroccans – will kidnap you. Moroccans are filthy, dirty people who will steal your money and rape you.'

'You said no one would hurt me!' I wanted to shout at him. But I stayed silent, and as I looked down at the road that was speeding past beneath the wheels of the car, I considered for a moment opening the door and throwing myself out. And then I thought of my mother and how she would live for the rest of her life believing whatever story Kas told the police and would never know what had really happened to me. I think, too, there was still a part of me that couldn't believe that what he was talking about would ever become a reality.

That afternoon, back at Kas's flat, he gave me my mobile phone and told me to call my mother. He'd already told me what to say, as well as what would happen if I said anything different, and he stood beside me as I dialled the number. Mum answered on the first ring and I could hear the relief in her voice as she said, 'I'm *so* glad you've rung, Sophie. I was worried when you didn't answer my text, although Steve said it was just because you had more exciting things to do than phone your mother. And I know that's true. But, even so, I couldn't help being a bit worried. Is everything okay?'

'Yeah, everything's fine, Mum,' I told her, biting my lip to stop myself bursting into tears. I turned my head away from the phone, coughing to cover up the tremor in my voice, and as Kas laid a warning hand on my arm, digging his fingers painfully into my flesh, I took a deep breath and tried to sound cheerful as I told my mother, 'In fact, I'm having an amazing time and ...' I hesitated and closed my eyes. Once I'd said the words Kas had told me to say, there would be no going back. I would cut myself off from my family and from any chance I might have of getting away from him – although, in my heart, I knew I'd passed that point already.

'In fact,' I said again, 'I've got some great news. Guess what?' As I ran the back of my hand over my face to wipe away the tears, I thought for a moment that the words I was screaming inside my head were going to burst out of my mouth – and then God knows what Kas would do to me. But, instead of shouting, 'Help me, Mum! I'm trapped here and I need you,' I fought back the tears and said, 'I've decided to stay here in Italy, with Kas. We're planning to go travelling together later. So ... So I won't be coming home for a while.'

'You're going to stay there?' My mother sounded shocked, and when she spoke again I could tell she was crying. 'But, darling, what about … What about your job?' She paused for a moment before adding hastily, 'I'm pleased for you, of course. If you're happy with Kas, that's great. It's just …'

'I have to go now, Mum,' I interrupted her. 'Sorry. I'll call you again soon.' I hated myself for hurting her. There was a tight pain in my chest and as Kas reached across and took the phone from my hands, I broke down and began to sob.

Much later, I discovered that my mother had tried to convince herself that her sense of disquiet was really just hurt feelings because of the ease with which I seemed to be able to walk away from my family. She'd tried to accept what I'd told her and be happy for me, although when she told my sister, Emily, 'Sophie's going to stay in Italy,' and Emily burst into tears and wailed, 'I want her to come home. I don't want her to be away,' Mum had cried too. But she knew Steve was right when he said, 'Sophie's young. She's enjoying herself, having fun. It's what you want for her. I know how close the two of you have always been, but let her go, love. She'll be back in touch when all the excitement dies down a bit. And even if she ends up marrying the man, Italy isn't exactly on the other side of the world' – although, for me, it might just as well have been, because the world I'd been forced to live in was not one I had even imagined existed.

I've always phoned my mother at least once every day, and I continued to call her almost daily for the first few days because Kas wanted to keep everything as normal as possible to avoid raising anyone's suspicions. But, after a while, as he became more violent towards me, I found it increasingly difficult to sound 'normal' when I spoke to Mum and, gradually, I phoned her less often, until several days would sometimes pass before I answered her text and voice messages.

It must have been hard for my mother when the close relationship we'd always had seemed to come to such an abrupt end. But she told herself that her misgivings – about whether I was really happy and everything was all right – were due to the fact that what I'd done was so out of character, and that she should be happy I'd had the confidence to spread my wings and start a new, independent life away from home.

I had other messages too, from friends as well as from my sister and brothers, and before I answered them, Kas would say to me, 'Do not say anything to raise anyone's suspicions. Act normally. Do not mess up.' So I'd speak quickly, always apparently with little time to spare because I was just about to go out, and I'd tell them how great everything was and how much I was enjoying myself. Then I'd drop the phone into Kas's outstretched hand and wait for him to tell me what to do next.

After I'd spoken to my mother that first day, I tried again to reason with Kas. 'Couldn't I go back home for just a few days?' I asked him. 'I need to tie things up and say goodbye to people. I'm supposed to give a month's notice at work, and I can't simply walk out on them.'

But he just sneered at me as he said, 'You're always such a timid little mouse. Why are you so frightened of these people? They wouldn't bother about letting *you* down. They wouldn't go out of their way to help *you*. You live in this little world where you're always running around doing what other people tell you to do. You go to work because it's what you think you *should* do. You're so conventional. But the truth is that no one gives a shit. It's just a job.'

It wasn't 'just a job' to me, though. Not wanting to let people down or feel that anyone had a reason to think badly of me was part of *me*. And I *really* wanted to see my sister and brothers, if only just to let them know that I would never willingly walk out of their lives and forget about them. Our father had walked away from us without a backward glance, and I couldn't bear to imagine how hurt they must feel now that I'd apparently done the same thing.

At about 7 o'clock on that Monday evening, Kas handed me some clothes and told me to put them on. I'd been crying and he slapped my head as he said, 'And for God's sake, woman, tidy up your hair. Look at the state of you! Who in their right mind would want to pay money to have sex with someone whose hair looks like the nest of a bird?'

I cried again, silently, as I put on the clothes he'd given me – the black skirt made of shiny, cheap material that was too short and flared out too much at the bottom, the ugly top and the hold-up stockings under knee-high boots. Then I applied make-up in exactly the way Kas told me to do it, brushed my hair until it was as sleek and neat as he liked it to be, and looked in the mirror in the bathroom at someone else's reflection.

I felt stupid, like a child trying on dressing-up clothes, but when I walked into the living room, Kas put his hand on my shoulder, turned me round slowly and, using the first nice words he'd spoken to me all day, said, 'My little mouse. How frightened you are and how beautiful you look now.' For a moment, I felt almost a sense of pleasure, because instead of shouting at me or hitting me, or looking at me with cold, cruel disgust as he'd done so many times during the last 24 hours, he'd praised me, which meant that I'd finally managed to do something right – even if it didn't feel right to me at all.

It was dark and getting cold by the time we drove down the hill to the main road. Kas stopped the car beside an area of broken concrete that ran along the edge of the road in front of some derelict buildings, and a girl stepped forward from the shadows. She smiled at Kas as she leaned in through the open window of the car to kiss him on both cheeks. Then she looked at me appraisingly, said something to him in Italian and they both laughed.

'Cara will show you what to do,' Kas told me, 'but just for a couple of nights. So pay attention, because after that you'll be on your own.'

I followed the girl to her car, which was parked down the side of one of the dark, broken-windowed buildings, and a few minutes later we were driving down the road as she added her instructions to the multitude Kas had already given me.

'You are here sometimes,' she said, in stilted English, pointing to a patch of grass under a single, leafless tree. 'If the *Carabinieri* see you at your other place, you go here.'

For a moment, my heart stopped beating and I thought I was going to faint. 'The *police*?' I said. 'But what will *happen* if the police see me?'

'It's normal,' she told me, lifting her hands off the steering wheel as she shrugged. 'They tell you "*Vai!* Go!" Or they take you to the *stazione* for a few hours. But it's not a problem.'

Tears had started to roll down my cheeks and when Cara noticed them, she shrugged again. Clearly, the prospect of being taken to a police station held no shame or dread for her. Later that evening, she told me that she used to work in a bakery, but had given up her job to work on the streets voluntarily to earn the money to pay her boyfriend's legal fees when he'd been sent to prison for kidnapping a girl and forcing her into prostitution. And she laughed as she told me, 'It's better money than selling bread, and more exciting.'

She made me memorise her phone number, as Kas had done, telling me, 'Call me if you have problems.' And then she took me to the spot where she would wait with me for customers that night.

After parking her car on a narrow dirt track, out of sight of passing motorists, she led the way back to the main road, where she stood, calmly confident, beside me while I tried to concentrate on not being sick. The temperature had dropped abruptly in the last hour or so, and although I was wearing a jumper over the hideous top, I was shivering violently – both with cold and with fear. Suddenly, Cara turned and started walking back towards the car, ignoring me when I called frantically after her and then disappearing into the darkness.

I stood alone under the single streetlight at the side of the busy main road, trying to control the panic rising up inside me and praying that no car would stop, and I almost cried with relief when I saw her running up the track towards me again. In her hand, she was holding a white tracksuit top, which she told me to put on. Then she placed her hands on my shoulders, turned me round so that I was facing her and pulled up the zip, just like my mother used to do when I was a child. My eyes filled with tears, and at that moment, a car drew up beside us and Cara pushed me towards it. 'I *can't*. Please Cara,' I whispered to her. But she'd already turned away.

As I bent down to look in through the car's open window, I felt as though I was outside my own body, watching myself, and all I could think was, *How is this going to happen? How am I going to do this? I can't.* And then, just as I felt Cara's finger poking me sharply in the back, the stranger asked me '*Quanto?*' I took a deep breath and answered '*Trenta Euros*', and to my horror, he shrugged his shoulders and said 'Okay.'

I stood with my fingers still resting on his open window, swallowing the sour bile that was flooding into my mouth, and prayed that I wasn't actually going to vomit. My legs felt like leaden weights and I could hear a voice inside my head screaming *No!* And then Cara said '*Vai.* Go!' and I walked around the car, opened the door on the passenger's side and got in beside a man I didn't know.

As I pressed my body against the door and gripped the armrest so tightly my fingers ached, he must have wondered what was wrong with me. But he just shot me a quizzical glance and then asked in Italian, 'Where? Where do we go?' With my heart pounding, I tried to remember what Cara had told me just a few minutes earlier. 'Go straight,' I said, hoping I'd pronounced the Italian word correctly. 'Then left.' I sounded like a terrified, timid robot, and perhaps he was beginning to wonder why he'd agreed to pay 30 Euros to have sex with someone who was obviously crazy.

He was young – probably not much older than me – and as he drove he asked my name and where I was from. Kas had created a persona for me, a ridiculous story I was supposed to tell anyone who asked any questions. So I told the man I was Russian, my name was Jenna and I was working as a prostitute because I needed to send money home to my family in Russia. I spoke in broken English, in what was supposed to be a Russian accent, although it sounded nothing like one. As the words tumbled out of me, I began to think that if I could make this man believe I was Jenna, perhaps I could believe it too – if only just enough to be able to detach myself from the reality of what was happening.

When he stopped the car at the spot I directed him to – the one that Cara had pointed out to me earlier – the voice in my head began to shriek, *I can't do this. Oh God, what am I going to do?* For a few horrible seconds, I sat there in total silence, and then I started to fumble in my pocket for a condom. I'd never put a condom on anyone before and I didn't have any idea how to do it. The worst part of it all, though, was asking, '*Bocca* or *fica*?' And as I whispered the words, the sour taste filled my mouth again.

'*Bocca*,' the man answered, and I felt a surge of relief – until I realised that the moment had really come and I was going to have to do what he was expecting me to do. The thought flashed through my mind to tell him I wasn't what I seemed to be. I wasn't Russian and I didn't have a poor family dependent on my ability to trade sex for money. I was a 'nice' girl from England, who'd come to Italy to visit a man she thought was her friend but who had threatened her family and forced her to work as a prostitute. Then, as I remembered what Kas had told me about sending people to check up on me, so that I would never know whether a man who stopped his car beside me was really a client, I could see in my mind the look that had been on his face when he'd said, 'And you wouldn't want to be responsible for what would happen to your precious brothers then.'

So, instead of bursting into tears and begging, 'Please, *please* help me. I've been kidnapped and I can't do this,' I took the condom out of its packet, explained my awkward fumbling by telling the man 'It's my first time', and then did what he'd paid me 30 Euros to do.

As I tugged – awkwardly and with shaking fingers – at the zip in the man's trousers, I felt a surge of almost over-powering disgust at the thought of the intimate and very private act I was about to perform on the total stranger sitting beside me in his car. Then I closed my eyes and forced my mind to focus on the dark, empty space that seemed suddenly to surround me.

Afterwards, I handed him some tissues and while he cleaned himself up and refastened his trousers, I turned away so that he wouldn't see my tears. Slowly, I could feel my fear and self-disgust being replaced by a heavy, dull sense of shame – and that's when I realised with a sick feel-ing of horror that he hadn't actually paid me at all. I'd been so anxious to remember everything I was supposed to do, and so frightened by the thought of what Kas would say and do to me if I got anything wrong, I'd forgotten the most important thing of all – to make sure I got the money first. Luckily, though, when I asked him for my money, the man reached into his pocket, opened his wallet and handed me some notes, which I stuffed inside my boots, as Kas had told me to do. Then I sat in the car, numb and mute, while he drove me back to where Cara was waiting for me.

'How is it?' she asked me. 'It's okay?'

'Yeah, okay,' I told her. And in some ways it was, because the first time was over and I knew that, in future, 'okay' was going to mean something completely different from what it had ever meant before.

More cars came after that, and more men gave me more money, which I pushed down into my boots as I directed them to 'my spot'. And each time I performed the same horrible, disgusting act with a stranger, I felt a little more like Jenna – who was doing what she had to do to help her family – and a little less like Sophie, who lived in a nice flat in the centre of Leeds, had a good job and a mother, step-father, sister and brothers who loved her and who would not in a million years have believed it if someone had told them what she was doing.

I'd been with four men by the time a silver-coloured Mercedes pulled up beside us, and I was just about to walk round to the open window when Cara put a hand on my arm and said, 'We can't go with him. Say no.'

'What do you mean? Why not?' I asked her, my heart beginning to race.

'Just say no,' she hissed at me, and when I still hesitated, she stepped towards the car herself and said firmly, 'No! *Vai via!*'

I felt myself blushing with embarrassment because she'd spoken to him so rudely – a reaction that didn't strike me as ironic until much later – and then I held my breath and waited to see what the man would do. But in the end he just swore at her and drove away.

'What was wrong?' I asked Cara. 'Why did you tell him to go?'

'He's bad,' she answered, shrugging and pulling a face. 'He's a bad man. Remember this car and this face. Do not go with him – *ever*.' And the warning I could hear in her voice made me afraid in case I didn't recognise him if he came again.

Some of the men who stopped their cars beside us drove off when I told them the price, and then – eventually, inevitably – one of them said he wanted full sex. I hesitated, but when I looked at Cara she just nodded irritably. So I walked round to the passenger door and got into the car.

As the man drove down the road, following my directions, all I could think was, *This is it. Oh my God. This isn't pretend. I'm not Jenna, I'm Sophie, and this is really happening to me.* I turned to look out of the window beside me, hiding my tears while I prayed that *something* would happen so that I didn't have to go through with it. I knew, though, that I mustn't let him see my fear or realise I didn't know what I was doing and, with the voice in my head still repeating the words *You have to get a grip on yourself*, I wiped my hand across my face just as he asked me my name.

When he stopped the car and I couldn't push my seat back, so that he had to do it for me, I almost gave in to the panic that was building up like a tidal wave inside me. Somehow, though, I managed to detach myself just enough to be able to shut my mind to what I was doing – until he tried to touch me. I could pretend – almost – that I couldn't feel the weight of his body as he lay on top of me, pushing me down on to the seat and crushing my thighs painfully with his knees. And I could turn my head away so that the acrid smell of his breath didn't make me gag. But I knew I wouldn't be able to bear it if he touched me. I hated the thought of anyone putting their hands on my body and I could see he was startled when I almost shouted at him, 'It's not allowed. You can't do that.'

Afterwards, I gave him the tissues and lay there for a moment, thinking, *This is what I am now. This is what I'm going to have to do. I can't get away from it. I can't escape. Where would I go? Who could I tell?* I felt almost sullen, like a petulant child who'd been made to do something she didn't want to do, although without any simple, child-like sense of resentment or injustice. Instead, I was completely numb – both mentally and physically – and I was barely aware of what I was doing as I pulled up my pants and straightened my clothes. Then, as the stranger I'd had sex with drove me back to the place where, just a few minutes earlier, he'd picked me up, I stared miserably out of the window of his car and saw nothing but darkness.

From 8 o'clock in the evening until 5 the next morning, I was almost literally going round in circles: waiting with Cara at the side of the road, being picked up by someone and driven to 'my spot', then back again to the pick-up point, where I'd start the whole process all over again. And, gradually, as the minutes and then the hours ticked by, my mind shut down and the numbness almost obliterated the fear and revulsion.

By the time Cara dropped me off at the bottom of the hill and I walked up the road to Kas's flat, I was so tired I could hardly think. Kas was waiting for me and when he'd counted the money I handed to him, he said, 'Three hundred and fifty Euros is okay for the first night, but after tonight such a small amount won't be acceptable. Monday to Wednesday, you need to be earning at least six to eight hundred Euros; a thousand or more on Thursdays to Sundays. Now go to bed. You look terrible.' Then he threw the money on to the table beside the sofa and turned up the volume on the television.

I think I'd been with 10 men that night, which, to me, seemed like a very high number indeed. But although I was disgusted by what I'd done, I think I'd almost hoped that Kas might praise me for having earned as much as I had. In fact, though, his criticism didn't really matter, because by that time my mind had shut down so completely that I don't think I was capable of feeling anything at all.

In the bathroom, I pulled off the ridiculous knee-high boots, the shapeless black mini-skirt and the horrible top and stood under the shower, feeling the water cascade down on my head and watching it swirl around my feet before disappearing into the drains beneath the city. I still hadn't moved when Kas came into the bathroom and as he stood watching me silently, I felt a sudden surge of emotion and begged him, 'Please. *Please*, Kas, don't make me do it again. I can't.' I was exhausted and I didn't care if he shouted at me or even hit me. But I hadn't anticipated the intensity of his rage.

Without any warning, he flew across the room, grabbed me by the throat and started banging my head against the tiled wall of the shower. I was gasping for breath, taking in great gulps of water, while Kas was screaming at me, 'Who do you think you are? You do not question what I tell you to do. How *dare* you question me? Have you failed to listen to a single word I've said to you? Do you not understand that it isn't your place to tell me what you can and can't do? You will do what I tell you to do. This is the way it will be from now on. You don't even have to think for yourself: you simply have to do what you're told.'

I was choking; it felt as though my lungs were filling up with water, and when he loosened his grip for a moment, I began to gasp as I tried to catch my breath. I was still spluttering when he grabbed my throat again, slamming my head back against the wall and shouting, 'You fucking try and do anything and then you'll see what I'll do to you. If you try to go anywhere or tell anyone, I'll *kill* you.'

When he finally dragged me out from underneath the shower, my lungs felt as though they were bursting and there was a tight band of pain across my forehead. But as soon as I could breathe enough to be able to speak, I whispered, 'I'm frightened. I don't want to be out on the streets. If I have to do it, can't I do it in a house?'

'Are you fucking stupid?' he yelled, punching the side of my head with his fist so that I would have slipped and fallen if he hadn't already twisted his fingers into my wet hair. 'Is there anything in your head except sawdust? Do you think someone wants to hurt you? Why? Why would they bother? All they want to do is fuck you.'

After that first night, I worked seven nights a week, from eight in the evening until five or six in the morning. I would have, on average, about 25 customers every night – the minimum was 18 and the most, one night, was 34 – and it wasn't long before my spirit was crushed. I was so weary that nothing seemed to matter and I didn't care whether I was alive or dead.

Sometimes when I got back to the flat in the early hours of the morning, Kas was angry, and sometimes he talked to me almost normally about himself and his life. At the time, it never crossed my mind to doubt whether the things he told me were true – I believed them without question, just as I believed everything he said. But looking back on it now, I don't think he ever told the truth about anything.

He said he was 17 when he started smuggling – first, people from Albania to Italy, then guns, and then drugs from Holland, until he realised there was less risk involved in simply dealing drugs within Italy itself. He claimed to be the biggest drug dealer in the area, and told me, 'I almost always work on my own. Other people are stupid and get you into trouble, so it's better to rely only on myself. That way I know I'll be safe.' He stroked my hair as he added, 'But you, my little mouse, I know that you will never let me down. I know I can trust you. You won't get me into trouble, will you?' And as I shook my head and whispered 'No', I felt a small, bizarre thrill of pleasure at the thought that perhaps, despite everything, he really did love me.

Sometimes, when he threatened me and told me what he'd do if I disrespected him, I'd say to myself, *He's just angry because I made a mistake. But he won't do that. He loves me.* And each time he hit me and shouted, 'What's the matter with you, woman? I don't know what your problem is. What I'm asking you to do is just normal. Why are you so stupid?', I'd cry and hate myself for *always* making mistakes and getting everything wrong. Because I knew that Kas's anger with me was justified and he was right: I was far too stupid to deserve to be loved by anyone.

Chapter 7

I hadn't been in Italy very long before Kas had changed everything about me, until there didn't seem to be anything left of Sophie – at least, nothing I recognised and could connect with – and I'd sometimes stand in front of the bathroom mirror and not be able to see my reflection at all.

Although I did everything Kas told me to do, it seemed that, however hard I tried to get things right, I always did something wrong. And as even the smallest, apparently most insignificant mistake would send him into a rage, I was always frightened. Most of the time, I walked around like a zombie, with my mind almost completely empty, because I quickly learned that if I didn't think, I didn't feel so much, and then I was less aware of the profound sense of misery that otherwise stayed with me every minute of every day and every night.

I never spoke unless Kas spoke to me, and when he asked me simple questions that I couldn't answer – usually because I was too anxious to be able to focus my thoughts – I told myself he was right and I *was* becoming more stupid with every day that passed. Before long, I could barely think or act independently, although that didn't really matter because all I needed to do was work on the streets every night, force down as much as I could of whatever food Kas banged down on the table in front of me, and then sleep until it was time to get up and start the whole thing all over again.

On the rare occasions when I went out in public with Kas, I had to wear a tracksuit and a cap pulled down over my eyes so that no one would recognise me and so that I wasn't able to look directly at other people. Above all, I wasn't allowed to look at men. According to Kas, one of the two friends of his who I'd met at the café during my first weekend in Italy had said afterwards that I kept looking at him in a suggestive way. 'I *didn't*. I swear I didn't,' I told Kas. But he hit me and shouted at me anyway, until I began to wonder if perhaps I was wrong.

After that first weekend, I slept alone in a single bed in Kas's bedroom. Sometimes, he'd wake me up and make me lie with him on the sofa in the living room while he stroked my hair and called me his 'beautiful little mouse'. He only very rarely wanted to have sex with me, but when he did, although the act itself didn't give me any pleasure – it felt no different from having sex with a customer – it meant that I'd done something right, something Kas approved of. And obtaining Kas's approval had quickly become my single most important goal.

Of all the threats and warnings Kas constantly shouted at me, there were two things he said more often than any others: 'This is what you have to do if you love someone: you have to make sacrifices' and 'You see what I'll do to you if you disobey me'. And as well as the criticisms, there was a seemingly endless list of rules – things I wasn't allowed to do or must do in a certain way. In fact, there were so many rules that although I would never have dreamed of disobeying any of them deliberately, I was always terrified of accidentally making a mistake.

It was a long time before I first thought to wonder whether Kas did the things he did as a means of escaping from a hard life. I don't really know anything about his background and upbringing – particularly as the few things he *did* tell me were probably untrue. But I'm pretty sure he did what he did for the love of money, and because there was no need for him to work himself when he could so easily cajole, threaten and coerce other people into earning money for him.

Until the Sunday evening of the first weekend I spent with Kas in Italy, it would never have entered my mind to doubt the fact that he was a sympathetic, compassionate man. I soon discovered, however, that he was, in reality, a totally ruthless, self-serving bully with the heart of a criminal, who was so completely and utterly focused on what *he* wanted that he was unable to empathise with anyone.

Even when I was working on the streets as a prostitute, when no one in their right mind could possibly have believed that he loved me, he sometimes told me that he did. And although I clung to the hope that it might be true, I think I knew that he was incapable of love and that I was merely a means to an end, someone he could use and abuse and didn't care about at all.

Another of Kas's recurring themes whenever I dared to complain about anything, however mildly, or begged him not to make me do something that horrified or frightened me even more than all the other things he made me do, was 'thinking about people who are worse off than you are' – which was ironic really, in view of the fact that the only person who mattered to him at all was himself. Apart from anyone he could manipulate and use for his own ends, he had absolutely no interest in or sympathy for other people. So when he shouted the phrase at me, it often seemed as though he was just repeating something that perhaps his mother used to say to him when he was a child.

On the third night, when I worked alone, without Cara, I constantly had to fight the desire to crouch down behind the low wall at the back of the petrol station and hide until it was time to go home. But I knew there was nothing any of the men who stopped their cars beside me could possibly do to me that would be as bad as what Kas would do if I went back to the flat without any money. So I'd already had several customers in the couple of hours since he'd dropped me off, when a car pulled up beside me and two policemen jumped out. For some reason – perhaps because of the angle at which the vehicle had approached me – I hadn't noticed until it was too late the word *Carabinieri*, which was written in large letters on either side of the car, and my heart began to race as I tried to remember what Kas and Cara had told me to do in a situation like this.

One of the policemen walked quickly towards me, shouting and waving his arms in the air, while I just stood there, shaking and too frightened to move. When he was close enough, he suddenly reached out his hand and snatched my bag from my arms, breathing cigarette smoke into my face as he yelled, '*Vai via! Non scopa!* [Go away! No fucking!]' Still shouting at me, he began to search through my bag, his large hands pushing packs of tissues and condoms out on to the grass at my feet. I crouched down to scoop them up, but he grabbed the shoulder of my jacket, pulled me to my feet again and said, '*Vai!* No pretty woman here.'

I kept my eyes down – trying to avoid antagonising or 'disrespecting' him – and said nothing, even when he slammed my bag back into my arms and shoved me against the side of the car. He held me there with one hand, while he used the other to open the rear door, then he bellowed into my face '*Andiamo!* [Let's go!]' and pushed me down on to the back seat. As the car swerved out onto the road, the other policeman said something in Italian and they both laughed. I felt anxious and vulnerable. No one except the two policemen knew where I was – not that anyone would care about what had happened to me if they did. Then I remembered what Kas had told me to do.

Slowly, and making as little movement as possible, I reached into my bag, took out my mobile phone and, holding it on my lap, sent Kas a message containing the single word 'flic'. Then I deleted the number from the call log, slipped the SIM card into the pocket of my jacket and dropped the phone back into my bag. Instantly I felt better. Kas would know what to do; he'd make sure nothing bad happened to me. But what if he was angry with me for having allowed myself to get picked up by the police? What if the policemen searched me and found the SIM card with Kas's phone number on it? My heart started to race again and I cursed myself for having been so stupid and for not noticing the police car as it approached.

It took about 15 or 20 minutes to drive to the police station, and neither of the policemen spoke to me before we got there. After they'd led me to an interview room, one of them told me, curtly in English, 'Coat off; and boots,' and I had to bite my lip to stop myself bursting into tears of humiliation and self-pity.

I'd only ever seen the inside of a police station on television, and I'd never been in trouble of any kind before – it wasn't something I'd have dreamed in my wildest nightmares would ever happen to me. And as I bent down to unzip the cheap white boots, my mother's face flashed into my mind and I had to stifle a choking sob. I could feel my cheeks flushing red with shame at the thought of how shocked and mortified she'd be if she could see me – standing in a police station in a foreign country having been picked up on the streets for working as a prostitute. No wonder the policemen were treating me like crap.

I'd been so anxious to do what they told me and so focused on wanting to show them I wasn't the type of girl they assumed I was and I wasn't going to cause any trouble, that I'd forgotten about all the money inside my boots. As it fluttered out on to the floor, I began to snatch it up and stuff it into the pockets of my jacket, like some frenzied beggar, and then my heart sank as I realised there was now no way they would believe me when I denied what I'd been doing at the side of the road.

One of the policemen began to shout at me, 'You are disgusting. You will be sent back to your own country and then everyone will know what you have done in Italy. You have put shame on your family.' Then he pointed to some chairs and a small metal table, which were the bleak little room's only furniture, and as soon as I sat down, he started firing questions at me. 'What is your name? When did you come to Italy? Where are you living?' And I told them the story Kas had told me to tell and gave the address he'd made me learn.

'So, if we take you to this address, you will unlock the door with your key and go inside?' the other policeman asked me. And I tried to look confident as I wiped my hands on my skirt and whispered, 'Yes, of course.'

For a split-second, it flashed across my mind to tell them the truth. But then I heard Kas's voice in my head saying, 'You will never know whether people are who they say they are. You will never know who is working for me. Do you know what I will do to you if you disrespect me?' And I realised I could never dare trust anyone or ask for anyone's help.

They kept me at the police station for a couple of hours and when they told me to leave, I walked out of the door and into a town I didn't know. I thought about trying to hitch a lift from a passing car – maybe I could get lifts all the way back to England, or at least to somewhere far enough away so that I could phone my mum and Steve and they'd come and pick me up. I stood for a moment, imagining what it would be like to see their car driving along the road towards me. But I knew the idea was ridiculous, not least because, although I'd never hitchhiked in my life, I was pretty sure that doing it at 1 o'clock in the morning while dressed in a very short skirt and knee-length white boots wasn't a good idea. And, in any case, Kas had my passport and there *were* no cars – the streets were completely deserted.

I walked for a while to get away from the police station and then I sat on a bench next to a bus stop and faced the fact that there was only one person who could help me.

Kas answered his phone almost immediately and shouted, 'Where the fuck are you?'

'I got picked up by the police,' I sobbed. 'And I don't know where I am.'

'Don't you fucking cry, woman.' For a moment his voice was dangerously quiet, and then he was shouting again, '*You* wait! Just you wait and see what I'm going to do to you. How fucking stupid are you not to watch where you were being taken? And now you expect *me* to come and find you, with police everywhere. If I get picked up, it will be your fault and believe me, woman, then you'll really have something to make you cry.'

'I'm sorry,' I whispered. 'I was frightened. I didn't …'

'What can you see?' he snapped. 'Look around you. Think, woman, *think*.'

I was already used to his two-second rule – when he gave me just two seconds to answer a question before hitting me – but the more he harassed and bullied me, the less able I was to focus my mind and think of an answer or do whatever it was he wanted me to do. Luckily, though, I managed to describe where I was well enough for Kas to find me, and half an hour later I was sitting beside him in his car while he shouted at me, first in Albanian and then in English, that I was a 'mother-fucking bitch'.

'How fucking stupid are you?' he screamed. 'Are you trying to get me into trouble with the police? Is that it? Is *that* what you want to do?'

'No, no, of course not,' I whimpered. 'I'm sorry.'

'I don't know why I bother with you,' he sneered. 'Look at you! You're useless. How much money has your stupidity cost me tonight? Well, you're going back to work.'

I tried to cover up the sound of my indrawn breath by coughing, but Kas had heard it. Without turning his head, he lifted one hand from the steering wheel, reached across and slapped the side of my head as he said, 'You're such a frightened little mouse. You can't even do this one simple thing. You're a fucking waste of time. I know you're going to get me into trouble. I should get rid of you and do this with someone else.'

'I'm sorry,' I said again. 'It's just that I don't know what I'm doing.' And I prayed he couldn't hear the voice in my head that was screaming, *Please, please, please do it with someone else.*

'Do you think it's hard, woman?' Kas roared at me. 'All you have to do is open your legs. Someone fucks you, you move on. It's not fucking hard!'

Again, I wanted to shout at him, 'It *is* hard. Even just standing on the street is hard.' But all I said was, 'I'm frightened. Please don't make me go back tonight.'

'*Frightened?*' Kas's laugh was scornful. 'You're frightened of some stupid policeman? You're going to be scared off because of *one* policeman?'

'There were two of them,' I said. 'And they told me I wasn't to go back.'

'Oh, I *see*. Now I understand.' His voice was mocking. 'You're not going to go back because you've been *told* not to.'

'But what if they come again?' I said. 'What will happen to me if they pick me up again?'

He was right on one count, though, because being told not to go back was, for me, a good enough reason to stay away. I felt as though I was completely out of my depth: I was being forced to do something that went against all my instincts – quite apart from my morals – and I was scared. I began to cry, and that was when Kas seemed to lose control of his temper completely. Grabbing a handful of my hair, he banged my head against the window beside me, slamming it again and again into the glass until I felt faint and thought my skull was going to splinter. Then, suddenly, he let go of my hair and seized my throat, crushing my windpipe with his fingers until I couldn't breathe. I tried to pull his hand away, and just when I thought my lungs were going to burst, the world turned black.

The next thing I was aware of was Kas leaning over me, saying, 'Breathe, woman. *Breathe.*' He'd stopped the car at the side of the road and was holding my head in both his hands as he said, in a voice full of urgency, 'What have I done? Wake up, little mouse. *Please* wake up. We'll go to the hospital. We'll do whatever you want – *anything*. Just don't die. Please.'

My whole body seemed to be on fire, but as the air rushed into my lungs, I looked up into Kas's face and thought, *He does care about me. Everything is going to be all right now.* My head was pounding, but when I tried to speak he pushed me away, shouting, '*Don't* you fucking scare me like that again! Don't you test me, woman.' And as I cringed back against the car door, trying not to cry, he started the engine and said, 'You're no fucking good tonight. But you better sort yourself out by tomorrow. I'm not going through this again with you – you need to shape up.'

Later, as I lay in bed, sobbing silently, it felt as though someone was banging a drum inside my head, each beat sending a pulse of pain flooding across my skull. As the hours ticked by and I lay there, exhausted but unable to sleep, the thought suddenly struck me that maybe the two policemen were friends of Kas's who he'd sent to test me, to see if I'd take the opportunity to try to escape. The more I thought about it, the more likely it seemed that it was true, and, in fact, although I was picked up by different policemen on other nights, I was always taken to a police station just a few minutes' drive away rather than in another town, as happened on that first occasion.

Kas told me repeatedly, 'Don't think that the police are there to help you. Don't believe for one minute they're your friends. No one is your friend and no one you ever meet – not the police, other girls or any man – will ever help you.' And I knew he was right and that I could never trust anyone.

Sometimes, Kas would drop me off a short distance from 'my spot' and as I walked along the road I'd think, *Pull yourself together. Take it one day at a time and just concentrate on getting through this.* Then, as I stood waiting for cars to pull up beside me, I'd pray silently, *Please, please, please God, don't let anything happen to me. Just let me get through this night.* And every night I survived felt like another night when I'd somehow managed to dodge a bullet.

I think I'd almost forgotten that the reason I was working on the streets was, ostensibly, to pay off Kas's debt. I tried never to think about what might happen to me tomorrow, or the day after that, because when I did, all I could see was the same life stretching out endlessly ahead of me into darkness. Thinking about the future just made it harder to get through the day I was living at that moment. So I didn't know – or dare wonder – whether the time would ever come when I'd have had sex with enough men to have earned the money Kas owed.

By the time I finished working at around 5 o'clock every morning and walked to where Kas picked me up, the road would be almost empty of cars. He was forever telling me how important it was that I should keep checking to make sure I wasn't being followed, and how dangerous it was for him to risk being seen with me – which was ironic, considering I'd just spent the night standing alone in the dark waiting to have sex with total strangers. He'd often remind me, too, that if we were ever seen together, I must say I didn't know him and that he was just someone who was giving me a lift. But after the first couple of weeks he stopped picking me up at all, except very rarely – I suppose he was satisfied by then that I was so cowed and afraid of him I wouldn't try to escape – and I'd have to hitchhike, or ask my last customer to drop me off near the bottom of the hill that wound up to Kas's flat.

At home in England I wouldn't have dreamed of hitch-hiking under any circumstances, even in broad daylight, let alone on almost deserted roads in the early hours of the morning. But, then, never in my worst nightmares would I ever have imagined I might one day work as a prostitute, and it was surprising how quickly I adapted to taking risks, especially when it was a case of either hitchhiking or walk-ing miles when I was already cold and exhausted. And sometimes I'd think, *It doesn't really matter if someone does attack me. At least if I'm dead I won't have to do this anymore.*

As I was standing at the side of the road, I'd often think about my mother and wonder what she'd say if she could see what I was doing. To begin with, I still felt very much connected to her, but gradually, as my world contracted until it encompassed only Kas's flat and the streets where I worked, everything outside it lost its focus.

Surviving meant separating my mind from my body and trying to believe that I wasn't Sophie anymore; I was a Russian girl who was doing what she had to do to support her family and keep out of trouble. If I thought about anything else, I just got upset, and that made it harder for me to detach myself from what used to be my reality but was now my past. What I wanted and what I felt didn't matter anymore, because my sole purpose had become to earn money for Kas.

For the first couple of weeks, I wasn't making enough and I'd dread the moment every night when I had to stand beside Kas while he counted out what I'd given him. Every night he was angry with me, but I was going with every man who stopped and accepted the price I told him, and I just didn't know how I could do any more than I was doing. I began to think that maybe I just wasn't pretty enough for men to want to have sex with me. I certainly didn't *feel* pretty, standing at the side of the road shivering and nervous, like a skinny, timid little girl, and I knew I looked stupid in the clothes Kas made me wear. But nothing I could tell him made any difference, and he kept insisting I must be stealing from him and cheating on him with other men. I don't know if he really believed that, or whether it was just a way of making me try to do better, but he'd hit me when I cried and said, '*How* could I steal money from you? I'm giving you everything. *How* could I cheat? And *why* would I? These men are paying me to have sex with them – they don't want to have a relationship with me.'

Every night, as I stood at the side of the road waiting for my next customer, my mind would be torn completely in two: I'd be praying no cars would stop, so that I didn't have to have sex with anyone, and, at the same time, I'd be wishing more of them would, so that I could earn enough money to make Kas happy. Because if he was happy, he might not hit me and shout at me, 'How stupid are you? You can't even do one simple little thing.'

Another thing that enraged Kas was the fact that I found it so difficult to eat. I've never been a big eater, but I think part of the reason I lost my appetite then was because I was exhausted. Perhaps, too, not eating was a form of self-harming. Maybe I was punishing myself for doing the disgusting, horrible things I was doing every night. And maybe also it was a way of having autonomy over just one aspect of my life, which was otherwise entirely under Kas's control. At the time, though, I didn't think about the reasons why I couldn't eat, and even on the many occasions when Kas tried to force food into my mouth and shouted at me, I couldn't swallow more than a couple of mouthfuls without retching.

One day, he'd been out while I was asleep in the afternoon and when he came back he'd bought me a *panini* stuffed full of thick Parma ham and glutinous mayonnaise. 'Eat it!' he roared at me, as he always did, and my stomach immediately began to churn. It felt as though something solid was blocking my throat and as I took a bite and started to chew, I had to fight back the nausea rising up inside me. I could feel Kas watching me from the doorway of the kitchen, and suddenly he shouted, 'Eat it! You are disgusting. Do you not realise that there are people in this world who have nothing? Millions of people are literally starving to death and yet you refuse to eat good food that's put in front of you. You are a disgrace, woman.'

'I'm *trying* to eat it,' I told him, and as the tears spilled out on to my cheeks, he took two angry strides across the room, snatched the *panini* from my hands and started pushing it into my mouth, twisting the fingers of his other hand into my hair and wrenching my head backwards until I thought my neck was going to break. I began to retch and when he hit me across the side of my head, I pushed my chair away from the table and ran into the bathroom. After I'd been sick, I just wanted to lay my head on the cool tiles of the bathroom floor and go to sleep. But I knew Kas would be waiting for me.

He looked at me with an expression of contempt as I walked back into the kitchen. Then he pointed to the kitchen table, said 'Eat it' and left the room, and a few seconds later I could hear the sound of the television in the living room. Alone in the kitchen, I chewed and tried to swallow as much of the food as I could, and then I broke the rest into small pieces and hid them up my sleeves, before going back into the bathroom to vomit and flush away what I'd managed to secrete.

Perhaps by not eating I was trying to control just one aspect of my life, although if that *was* the case, it was subconscious and I certainly didn't realise it at the time. Inevitably, though, as I became thinner and more malnourished, I began to get one cold after another. Kas would just look at my puffy eyes and red nose with an expression of disgust and send me out to work as usual, although he did start making me eat bananas and spoonfuls of honey every day – both of which I've always hated and made me retch and throw up, so that he had to spoon in more.

One day, I was nibbling the end of a banana he'd just given me, trying to ignore my growing sense of nausea and think about something else, when he suddenly snatched it out of my hand and squashed it into my face and hair, shouting, 'Just look at you! You're like an animal. Do I have to do everything for you, woman? Can you do nothing for yourself? Are you so stupid you can't even eat a banana unless I help you?'

Sometimes I'd see the warning signs that meant his anger was about to erupt, and sometimes, as on that occasion, it flared up so abruptly and unexpectedly that it took me completely by surprise. And because it was so unpredictable, I was always on edge, like a frightened little dog waiting for its master to lash out and kick it across the room with the toe of his boot.

On another night, Kas told me to make pasta and tomato sauce for his dinner. I hated having to do anything like that. Because I was so afraid of getting even the smallest part of it wrong, I was constantly checking and double-checking until I was a twitching, miserable, nervous wreck. Although I thought I'd been able to cook perfectly well when I was at home, Kas had one day shown me, angrily, how to make this meal 'properly'. So, while the pasta was cooking in a pan of what I hoped was just the right amount of water boiling with just the right degree of vigour, I stirred the sauce and went over again in my head a list of all the ingredients I'd put into it, to make sure I hadn't forgotten to add anything.

Kas came into the kitchen just as I was straining the water from the pasta into the sink, and immediately my mind was buzzing with doubt. Was I using the right pan? Was I holding the strainer properly? Could I hear the sauce bubbling too vigorously on the stove behind me? If I turned my head to check, would some of the pasta slide out of the strainer and into the sink? What if didn't check and the sauce started to burn? Could I already smell burning?

With shaking hands, I put the strainer full of pasta on top of the empty pan on the stove, knocking the lid as I did so, so that it clattered on the work surface. I glanced quickly at Kas and whispered, 'I'm sorry.' But, to my relief, he just shrugged and sat down at the kitchen table. *It's going to be all right*, I told myself. *He's in a good mood, otherwise he'd have shouted at me because of the noise.* Even so, as I walked very slowly and carefully across the kitchen carrying the plate of pasta and freshly made tomato sauce and put it down on the table in front of Kas, I still held my breath and prayed, *Please, please don't let me have done this wrong.*

My heart was thumping as I watched him pick up his fork and take a mouthful of the food. When he raised his eyes to look at me, I couldn't read his expression. Was he pleased? Did he like it? Had I added too much salt? Had I overcooked the pasta?

Suddenly the room was filled with the sound of his anger, and I heard myself whimper like a frightened animal as he pushed the table away and stood up.

'You *motherfucker!*' he bellowed at me. 'Are you trying to fucking kill me? What *is* this? I wouldn't give this disgusting slop to a dog! How many times do I have to tell you? Do you do this on purpose? Do you like to make me angry? What kind of person puts so much sauce on pasta?'

'I'm sorry. I'm sorry,' I snivelled.

'*Sorry?*' Kas roared. 'You *will* be fucking sorry!' And as he spoke he reached out his hand, lifted the plate off the table and hurled it at me.

Instinctively, I took a step backwards and as the plate smashed against the wall beside me, it sent out an explosion of broken china, pasta and thick tomato sauce. I was covered in it – it was in my hair and all over my clothes – and as I cringed and cowered against the wall, sobbing and trying to protect my head with my hands, Kas flew across the kitchen and grabbed me by my hair. He seemed to be completely out of control, kicking and punching wildly, like a large, violent child in the throes of a terrible temper tantrum. He shoved me up against the wall, grasping my throat so tightly with his fingers that I thought he was going to choke and kill me. But, instead, he started bashing my head against the tiles and screaming into my face, 'How fucking stupid are you?'

I thought my skull was going to explode and as my knees gave way, Kas lifted me off the floor by my neck and threw me down at his feet, kicking me again as he shouted, 'You fucking clean that up, you mother-fucking bitch!' He pushed the back of my head so that my face was pressed

117

against the floor and began to wipe the tiles with my hair, before dragging me to my feet again and roaring, 'Look at your fucking hair. Do you take no pride in yourself, woman?' Then, suddenly, he let go of me and walked out of the room.

Every inch of my body hurt and I could feel the blood pounding in my temples as I just stood there, too shocked to move. And I was still standing there when Kas walked back into the kitchen, holding in his hand an electric razor. I tried to get away from him, but my feet slipped and slithered on the dirty floor and as he reached out and grabbed my arm, he shouted at me, 'I cannot stand any longer to look at this messy hair. I am going to cut it all off. You are *disgusting*. You're like an animal.' And that was exactly how I felt.

But instead of cutting my hair, he pushed me away from him and said, in a voice thick with disgust, 'Just look at you, shaking like a frightened little mouse. Get out of my sight. Go on. Clean up this mess and then go.'

So I scooped and scraped the food from the walls and floor and cleaned the kitchen, checking and re-checking for any traces I might have overlooked. And then I went into the bathroom, cleaned myself up, showered, changed my clothes and went to work on the streets, feeling angry with myself for having been so stupid as not to know how much sauce to put on a plate of pasta.

Chapter 8

Although I was always afraid of Kas, realising that I didn't have any control over what happened to me was almost a kind of release, and it wasn't long after the incident with the pasta sauce when I began to think, *If he does kill me, it doesn't matter. I don't care anymore.* I'd done well at school and had left with good A-level grades, and then I'd had a responsible job that required thought and a reasonable level of intelligence, but clearly, by any practical measures, I *was* stupid, and however hard I tried, I was never going to get things right. So it wasn't surprising Kas got angry with me when I couldn't do even the simplest thing.

One day, when I'd only been working on the streets for a few days, I did something that made him furious – there were so many things that I can't remember what it was –

and he drove me to a river, parked his car on the dusty grass separating it from the road, and told me to get out. Then he grabbed my arm, pulling me to the very edge of the black water, and said, 'If you ever disobey me again, that is where you are going to end up. I will kill you and put your useless, lifeless body in that river.' And I knew that he meant it.

For the first few nights when I was working on the streets, I would lie back on the seat of each new car and cry silently. But, gradually, I learned how to switch off the light in my mind so that it became dark and empty and I felt nothing – either physically or emotionally. After the first couple of weeks, I sometimes felt less vulnerable when I was working than when I was alone with Kas in the flat, never knowing what would be the next thing that would make him explode with anger. That sounds ridiculous, I know, but I began to have some regular customers who talked to me and were nice to me and with whom I felt almost at ease – in contrast to the many men who picked me up and frightened me, and some of whom asked me to do weird things, which I hated.

One night, I was picked up by an older man and as soon as I got into his car I felt scared. I didn't know why; there was just something about him I didn't like. I'd noticed it when I was talking to him through the open window, but I hadn't earned enough money that night and so I didn't have much choice if I was going to have any chance of avoiding being the target of Kas's fury.

The man kept touching me while we were having sex, and I told him – as I told all of them – that it wasn't allowed. Most men would apologise and stop immediately, but this particular man took no notice, even when I grasped his arm and pulled his hand away from my body. And then he snapped at me, 'If I can't touch you, how can I do this? Give me back my money.' I gave it to him immediately and breathed a sigh of relief when he dropped me by the side of the road near the petrol station. But as I stood there, waiting for the next car to pull up beside me, I thought about what had happened and realised I was being silly: I was performing what should have been intimate, loving, sexual acts with complete strangers, so it didn't really make much difference if they touched me. I think that was the moment when I stopped allowing myself to care about any of it.

I had customers of all ages, from early twenties to late sixties, or even older, and some of them were good-looking, which I hadn't expected. If I had ever given any thought in my previous life to what sort of men go to prostitutes – which I hadn't – I think I'd have assumed they were all scumbags. I certainly wouldn't have imagined that some of them would be 'normal' guys with girlfriends or wives and children. So it was strange to discover that most of them were ordinary, sometimes quite nice, men who apologised if they hurt me and who talked to me about their lives and their families. Sometimes, a man would ask how old I was and when I told him, he'd say, 'Ah, you're the same age as my daughter' – which seemed really creepy to me but never appeared to bother the men at all. It was a bizarre, surreal world and although nothing in it was familiar to me, nothing really surprised me, either.

But even with my regulars – the men I felt safest with – I didn't ever feel able to confide in any of them, because I never forgot that I couldn't trust anyone. I have a memory of being unnerved as a child when a teacher at school told me that God can see everything we do, even when we think we're all alone, and as I stood in the darkness at the side of the road, the thought would sometimes cross my mind that perhaps Kas could, too.

One night, a BMW pulled up beside me and I could see that there were two men inside it. I was always wary of flash cars anyway – especially BMWs and Mercedes – because they were the cars Albanians tended to drive. Kas told me repeatedly 'No Albanians' and he'd frightened me by saying, 'They won't care what they do to you or what happens to you afterwards.' But this particular night was another on which I hadn't made enough money, so my more immediate concern was what Kas would do to me, which probably made me less cautious than I might other-wise have been.

The two men paid me 50 Euros each, and when I insisted that one of them should wait at the side of the road while I went with the other, they shrugged their acceptance and the man in the passenger seat opened the door and got out.

I directed the driver to a spot further away than my usual one, which was just around the corner, because I was afraid that the other man might try to follow us. But already something didn't feel right, and when I had a chance to look at him more closely, I felt my stomach twist into a knot of fear as I realised he was Albanian.

Why hadn't I seen it immediately? I could hear Kas's voice in my head saying, 'He'll rape you, or he'll kidnap you and then kill you. How could you be so stupid?' Despite my fear, though, I knew I could have little influence over whatever was going to happen. *So what if he rapes me?* I thought. *What would it matter? I'm going to have sex with him anyway. The worst that can happen is that he kidnaps me – and then I'd just go from one situation that couldn't be any worse to another.*

At that moment, he turned and looked at me and the expression on his face made me think that perhaps things *could* be worse than they already were – a possibility that seemed to be confirmed when he stopped the car and told me he didn't want to have sex with me. Instead, he wanted me to sit beside him with my legs open while he stared at me. It was horrible. I felt embarrassed as well as scared, and it took every ounce of my willpower not to show that I was panicking.

'It's time,' I told him as soon as I thought I could get away with it. 'We have to go back.'

I was expecting him to refuse, or at least to argue, and I could feel every muscle in my body tensing. But he just shrugged, turned the key in the ignition and slewed the car across the road so that we were heading back towards where we'd left his friend.

Almost before he'd stopped the car, I jumped out and told his friend that I'd changed my mind and I wasn't going to go with him. 'Here, take your money,' I told him, fumbling in my boot to retrieve the 50 Euros he'd given me earlier and pushing the notes into his hand. He was standing so close to me that I could feel his breath on my face and as I took a step away from him, I realised that the other man had already got out of the car and was right behind me.

This is it, I thought. *It's over. They're going to do something horrible to me now.* I tried to focus on what Kas had told me so often: 'Don't ever let anyone see that you're afraid. As soon as they can see your fear, you've lost.' But it was difficult to hide it when my whole body was shaking violently. I was about half the size and certainly less than half the weight of the smaller of the two men, and I knew that if they intended to bundle me into their car, there was nothing I would be able to do about it.

Neither of them made any attempt to touch me though, as the man I'd been with said, 'Give me back my money.' I was so surprised that I answered without even thinking, '*No!* You've had your time. I can't. You have to go.' And then I used the Italian phrase that made most men who were considering messing with me change their minds: '*Il mio ragazzo è Albanese.* [My boyfriend is Albanian.]' It didn't work this time, however, and for a moment both of them just looked at me. Then the man said again, 'Give me my money,' and I held out the 50 Euros he'd paid me a few minutes earlier. It seemed a small loss if it meant they might leave me alone, although I didn't for one moment think that that would be the end of it and I expected them, at the very least, to rob me of the rest of the money I'd earned that night. So I was amazed when he snatched the notes from my hand and they both walked back to their car and drove off – the man in the passenger seat holding my gaze for a few seconds with a look on his face that seemed to say, 'Don't think you've seen the last of me. I'll be back for you.'

As soon as the car was out of sight, all the tension drained out of my body and I burst into tears. My knees gave way and I sat down abruptly on the dry, spiky grass to phone Kas and tell him what had happened.

'How fucking stupid are you?' he shouted at me. 'Why would you go with Albanians after everything I've told you? How many times do I need to say this to you? A child could understand the simple things I tell you, and yet you, woman, you can't even follow the most basic instructions.' He continued to rant at me for a while and then said, 'Tell me what they looked like. What sort of car were they driving?'

He'd drilled into me right from the start the need to make a mental note of the make and model of every car that picked me up and to memorise its number plate – which proved to be a great deal more difficult than it might sound. But I *was* able to describe this car and these men, and just a few minutes later, I saw Kas driving past in the direction they'd gone and I realised he must already have been somewhere in the area.

I was still standing at the side of the road when I heard what sounded like a car backfiring. I waited for Kas, but he didn't come, so I tried to push what had happened to the back of my mind and carried on working for the rest of the night.

Later, Kas told me he'd seen the BMW parked further down the road, where the men were talking to some girls, and he'd fired a warning shot at it – which must have been the sound I'd heard. He showed me his gun as he told me, 'Now perhaps you will understand that we are not playing games.' But as well as being frightened by the knowledge that someone as angry, unstable and unpredictable as Kas had a gun, I was appalled by what he'd done, because I knew the men would come back to make *me* pay for it.

And they did drive past slowly every now and then, just staring at me, and then, one night, at around 5 o'clock in the morning, when there was no one else left on the streets and I was about to go home, I recognised their car driving down the road towards me. With my heart racing, I slipped into the shadows and ran to the back of the petrol station, where I crouched down on the ground behind the low wall and tried to stifle the sound of my breathing. I knew that if the men got out of the car, I was dead. But, by some miracle, although they drove through the petrol station with the windows open, looking and listening for me, they didn't stop and, eventually, they drove away.

I'd learned my lesson, though, and after that I was more careful to look out for the national characteristics Kas had described to me – although I *did* wonder if the two Albanians would have continued to be quite so interested in me if Kas hadn't shot at their car.

I always dreaded having to go anywhere other than to one of 'my spots' with anyone and if someone said they wanted to take me to their house, I'd sit beside them in their car as they drove there, looking anxiously out of the window as I tried to memorise any landmarks that might help Kas find me if anything went wrong. As soon as I'd agreed to go with someone, I had to text him to let him know and to give him the registration number of their car, but I knew that, in reality, there would have been little he could have done in time if anyone *had* attacked me. So even though I could earn more money by going home with someone, which meant that Kas would be pleased – or, at least, less likely to be angry with me – it made me feel even more vulnerable and afraid than usual.

One night, I was picked up by a man who paid me 150 Euros to go to his flat with him. After we'd had sex and I told him his time was up, he gave me 150 more, and then another 50. Then he took off his watch and tried to make me take it so that I'd stay longer. But the truth was that, although I realised he didn't want to be alone and I felt sorry for him, I didn't want to be there at all, because I felt uncomfortable too, like a reluctant voyeur who was being forced to glimpse part of his life that no one else ever saw – and that I didn't want to see either. It made me even more nervous when he kept trying to make me take his watch, because I knew that just because he'd given me money didn't mean he was going to let me leave with it. But eventually he did drive me back to the petrol station, although, for reasons I didn't understand, I felt even more miserable than usual for the rest of the night.

On another night, a man took me on his boat on the lake. There were pictures of his wife on almost every flat surface and I couldn't imagine why he'd taken me there and why he didn't seem to see that there was anything wrong in what he was doing. I never did get used to the fact that most of the men who picked me up didn't appear to consider it to be a big deal and clearly had no sense of shame about it. The worst thing on that occasion, though, was that I kept remembering the day Kas had taken me to the river and told me how easy it would be for him to kill me and dump my body in its black water, and I realised that if the man decided to push me over the side of his boat, my body might never be found and no one would ever even know I'd been there.

Some men asked me to be their girlfriend; some even went so far as to say they wanted to marry me; and one who came quite regularly would beg me to go out to dinner with him and would be upset when I always said no. I was surprised by how completely divorced from reality they were, and by how easily they seemed to forget that the 'relationship' between us was purely a business one, and one that I was involved in entirely against my will – although I suppose there wasn't any reason for them to have known that.

What was even more surreal, though, was the fact that, in my old life, I'd probably have been friends with a few of the guys of my age. I wondered why some of them were there at all, why they paid for sex when there didn't seem to be any reason for them not to be able to have any girl they wanted. And I'd love to go back now to tell some of them what had happened to me and to explain that I wasn't really Jenna – particularly Marco.

I was frightened of Marco the first time he came, which was on the very first night I was working on my own near the petrol station. He was driving a BMW and although he told me he was Italian, I was afraid that he might really be Albanian. But he was nice to me and I found that I was quite glad to see him when he came again a few days later.

I'd been telling Kas for days that I was hopeless at doing a Russian accent and that no one believed my story, and he'd eventually agreed to let me drop my Russian persona. 'You can say you're from South Africa,' he told me, which was a huge relief, not least because it meant I could speak in my normal voice, as I knew that most people wouldn't be able to tell one English-speaking accent from another. And I was proved right, because once I became South African, no one ever again questioned the story I told them – although there was one guy who threw me into a panic when he asked me what I thought about apartheid and about the changes that had occurred in South Africa under Nelson Mandela!

But it meant that although I'd been pretending to be Russian the first time Marco came, I'd become South African when he came back. We were sitting in his car, just talking, when he suddenly looked at me with a puzzled expression and asked, 'Didn't you have a different accent last week? Aren't you Russian?'

'No, South African,' I told him brightly. Then I turned away from him and pretended to be re-fastening my boot as I muttered, '*Always* South African.'

'Oh, okay,' he said, and when I looked up at him again he shrugged his shoulders and grinned at me, and I had to laugh too.

Sometimes, Marco would come during the week just to check on me, and I always felt better when I saw his car and heard him call out '*Tutto bene?* [Is everything okay?]' Then, as he drove away again, he'd wave and say '*Ciao, bella*', and I'd really, *really* wish I could tell him the truth.

I had other regulars who did that too – just drove by from time to time to ask if I was okay – and I'd have to remind myself that they weren't my friends; they were men who paid me to have sex with them. Marco was different, though. I know it sounds silly, but he was respectful. He never tried to touch me and he treated me as though I was a girl he liked, rather than some sort of non-person.

We often just sat in his car and talked. He'd tell me about his work and about what he'd been doing since he last saw me and he'd try to get me to talk to him about myself. 'You're not like the other girls,' he told me. 'You're not cold and you talk to me like a friend. You look different too – *più elegante* [more elegant].' I laughed, and then tried to swallow the lump that had formed in my throat, because I really wanted to talk to him, but I knew I couldn't. I was already taking a huge risk, because if Kas ever happened to drive past and see us, he'd go crazy. But for a while, I'd sit in Marco's car and pretend that he really was my friend and that I was safe.

Kas often told me, 'Don't think that any of these men are your friends. They're not: all they want to do is fuck you and go home.' But when I was with Marco and, to a lesser extent, some of the other men who were nice to me, I'd think, *Kas is wrong. It isn't true that none of them cares about me.*

One night, I was picked up by an older, overweight man who told me he was a barrister. It seemed plausible, judging by the huge Bentley he was driving, and I recognised him immediately when he came back a week later with a friend. They both came again a few days after that, this time with a woman, and the barrister asked if I'd go back to his house with them.

'I'll give you 500 Euros,' he told me, and because I viewed everything in terms of how pleased or otherwise it would make Kas, I agreed.

I sat at the back of the car, next to the woman – who was the barrister's girlfriend – and as we drove to a very expensive and exclusive residential area just outside town, they all made polite conversation. After stopping to wait for a pair of wrought-iron electric gates to open, we drove into the driveway of an enormous house – the living room of which alone was bigger than the whole of Kas's flat.

It was a cold night, and although I was wrapped up in several jumpers and a jacket, I had virtually no body fat at all and nothing was able to keep out the chill that seemed to penetrate through my skin and into my bones. So I was glad to be inside in the warmth for a while, even though it meant being in a house miles from anywhere I was familiar with, in the company of three people who were clearly freaks and who wanted me to take part in some sort of weird sex party. But at least they were polite freaks and I didn't feel frightened or threatened by them, and I'd managed to text Kas to tell him where I was.

As soon as we walked into the house, the two men disappeared, and when they came back into the living room a few minutes later, wearing nothing but their socks, the barrister asked me if I'd like a drink. I was perched nervously on the edge of a very expensive-looking, cream-coloured leather sofa and I tried to look unfazed as I answered, 'No, just water.' So he poured wine for himself, his friend and his girlfriend and then she stripped down to her underwear and they all sat smoking and chatting as though everything was completely normal.

They spoke good English and when they asked me about myself, I told them my story – that I'd come to Italy from South Africa to earn money to send home to my family.

'It must be very hard for you,' the barrister's friend nodded sympathetically. 'But your family must be very grateful for what you're doing for them.'

In any normal world, it would have been a very strange thing for an almost totally naked man who was just about to have sex with me for money – and with his friend's girlfriend – to say. But in that world, everything was bizarre and yet nothing was extra-ordinary – because I *was* Jenna. In my mind, I actually *was* a young South African woman who was working as a prostitute so that her family wouldn't have to live with poverty and hunger. And that's how I got through all those nights – in people's houses and in cars on the dirt track near the petrol station – by detaching myself from Sophie and becoming Jenna, who *had* to do what she was doing because other people's lives depended on it. And that bit, at least, was true, because I had no doubt that if I didn't do exactly what Kas told me to do, he would carry out his threat to hurt my little brothers.

'And do you like doing what you're doing?' the barrister asked me, conversationally.

Are you out of your mind? I shouted at him, but only in my head.

'Not really,' I mumbled, looking down into my glass of water as I spoke.

'No, well, that's a shame,' he said – in the sort of tone you might use if someone told you they'd applied for a job at Starbucks but had had to accept one at Costa Coffee instead. 'But at least you have the satisfaction of knowing you're helping your family. Do you like Italy? What do you do when you're not working?'

If Alice in Wonderland had ever gone to a cocktail party, it would have been just like this, I thought, and for a moment I had to resist the urge to laugh. Three naked, or almost-naked, rich professional people were sitting in the elegant living room of a mansion in a suburb in Italy with a young woman they'd picked up on the streets, sipping wine from crystal glasses and asking her questions about her life and her 'chosen' line of work. And if that wasn't crazy enough, the truth of the matter – of which they were completely unaware – was that the prostitute was actually an English girl who'd been lured to Italy by someone she'd thought was her friend, but who was in fact an Albanian drug and people trafficker who was forcing her to work on the streets.

Suddenly the thought struck me that this was my chance. It was probably the best opportunity I would ever have to be able to tell someone the truth and escape from Kas. The man sitting beside me in his socks was a barrister and – despite his unusual sexual preferences – clearly someone who was wealthy and influential. I could tell him what had happened and he'd help me. But Kas had brainwashed me too well and, as the moment passed, I knew that I was too frightened to say anything to anyone. Perhaps what was even worse than the fear, though, was knowing that there would never be anyone I could turn to for help because I wouldn't ever be able to trust anyone.

Later, after the barrister, his girlfriend, his friend and I had all had sex in various combinations, I pushed the 500 Euros into my boots and sat in the Bentley beside the barrister while he drove me back to the petrol station. And I knew that nothing about any of it was really funny at all – in any case, I'd lost my sense of humour long ago. My life had been reduced to a handful of basic functions: I slept, got up, ate, had sex with strangers, tried to dodge the police and avoid getting attacked by anyone, went home, gave all the money I'd earned to Kas, and slept again. Above all, though, I did what Kas told me to do and tried to avoid making him angry with me. In some ways, it was all very simple and straightforward because I didn't really have to think. I just had to make sure I followed Kas's instructions – although that was never as easy as it might sound.

Despite the fact that Kas was a drug dealer and occasionally used cocaine himself, he was adamant when he told me, 'If I ever find out you've done any drugs, I'll cut your nose off. No one wants to fuck a junkie.' But no one ever did offer me drugs, and only one person ever asked to buy some off me, and then apparently found it hard to believe when I said I didn't sell them. It seemed odd to me – and strangely contradictory, as so many things were about Kas – that although he was quite happy to be a dealer, he would wind himself up into a fury at the very thought of my taking drugs. And then, one day, he told me he wanted me to sell wraps of cocaine.

'It's a missed opportunity,' he said, as though he was talking about some run-of-the-mill business venture rather than the serious criminal offence of drug dealing. 'All the men you're seeing want some pussy and they want some coke. You'll never be picked up for it because you won't be carrying enough to be viewed as a dealer. You just say it's for your own use.'

Until that moment, I'd believed things couldn't be any worse, but I knew that although I probably wouldn't get arrested for prostitution, I *would* go to prison if I got caught with drugs. And the fear must have been written on my face because Kas suddenly shouted at me, 'You're pathetic! I can see how frightened you are, and all because people tell you that you're not allowed to do something.' I knew there was no point pleading with him: he'd made up his mind and there was nothing I could do about it, but I dreaded going out to work that evening even more than I'd dreaded it before.

When I was dressed in my hideous work clothes, Kas called me into the living room, where the table was covered with little packages. I felt sick: I knew I couldn't do it; I'd mess it up – like I messed everything up – and I'd get caught, and then my mother would have to come and visit me in an Italian prison.

I began to cry and to beg Kas not to make me do it. 'I'm frightened,' I told him. 'Please, Kas. I don't know how to do this. I don't want to. Please, *please* don't make me.' Suddenly, he spun round, slapped me hard across the face and yelled, 'You haven't got the guts to do it, or the brains. Get out of my sight. You're an embarrassment – to me and to yourself. You're pointless. You'll only end up getting me into trouble because you're so stupid.' Then he rapped with his knuckles on the side of my head and said, 'There's nothing inside here except sawdust. That's why you can't think. Forget it. Go on, get out of my sight.'

And for once I was glad that I was stupid, if it meant not having to do something that, in my mind, was even worse than the things I was already doing.

One evening, when I was about to start getting ready to go out to work, someone banged on the front door of the flat. Kas was dealing a lot of drugs at that time and there were dozens of little wraps of cocaine on the table in the living room, which he started snatching up and pushing into a plastic bag, while I just stood there, frozen to the spot. Clearly, he wasn't expecting anyone, and the knock hadn't sounded friendly.

Kas had told me – repeatedly, as he told me everything – that if the police ever came, I was to say we didn't know each other and that I was a friend of a friend of his who he was allowing to stay at his place for a while. I wondered if this was the moment when I'd have to tell that story, and I was terrified at the thought of getting it wrong, of saying the wrong thing and getting Kas – and myself – into trouble.

Kas spun the top of the plastic bag into a tight spiral and tried to shove it into my hands, but I jumped back instinctively, dropping my arms to my sides, and he grabbed me roughly by the shoulders and snapped, 'Take it! Hide it. Go on. *Move*, woman!'

'Hide it *where*?' I whispered, closing my fingers around the bag and glancing nervously towards the door.

'Shove it inside you.' He pushed me towards the bedroom. 'And lock the fucking door.'

At that moment, a voice shouted '*Carabinieri!*' and I fled into the bedroom, closing the door silently behind me.

Fortunately, the two policemen didn't come into the flat, and for the next 10 minutes I sat, uncomfortably, on the bed, listening to the muffled sound of their voices and longing to light a cigarette. I couldn't make out what they were saying and Kas wouldn't tell me afterwards why they'd come. But when he eventually kicked the bedroom door and told me to come out, he was laughing, although his voice sounded contemptuous as he said, 'Fucking stupid bastards. Who do they think they are? Do they think they're going to catch *me*? They're *never* going to catch me! Fucking peasants, riding around in their police cars thinking they're so important.'

On another night, he made me sit in the kitchen and cut out little squares of plastic to wrap up a huge batch of cocaine. He reminded me – unnecessarily – about cutting off my nose if I even so much as sniffed in its general direction, and then he went into the living room to watch television.

Although it was a simple enough task, my palms were sweating and I was in a state of high anxiety, as I always was whenever Kas told me to do anything. But I was still taken by surprise when he came into the kitchen, snatched the scissors out of my hand and, pressing the tips into my cheek, shouted in my face, 'How stupid are you? Have you got sawdust in your head?'

I blinked and cringed away from him. But instead of hitting me, he picked up a piece of plastic paper from the table and cut out a square – which was almost identical to the ones I'd been making, except just a little larger. Then he grabbed me by the hair, wrenching my head back so that my neck twisted painfully, and held the square a couple of inches in front of my eyes as he said, angrily, '*This* is how you do it. This is not hard. How can you not be able to do this? Were you brought up by peasants?'

'No!' I wanted to shout back at him. 'I was brought up by people who weren't drug dealers and so never asked me to cut out little squares of plastic paper to wrap up cocaine.' But instead, I said quietly, 'I'm sorry. I didn't know. I haven't done this before.'

Kas's erratic, volatile temper was one of the most frightening things about him, and I was constantly trying – almost always unsuccessfully – to anticipate when and why he might fly into a rage, which meant that I was in a permanent state of anxiety. One minute he'd be okay – although it was rare for him to be actually calm and uncritical – and the next he'd be out of control, hitting me and shouting at me that I was stupid and that he didn't know why he bothered with me at all.

I still don't know if it was all a carefully calculated act to make me frightened of him – which it did – or whether he was actually mentally unstable. But it certainly seemed that almost everything I did was wrong, and even really minor mistakes – things that most other people would have considered too unimportant even to bother commenting on – seemed to send Kas into a frenzy of fury.

One day, he told me to pack away in a suitcase some clothes I didn't need, and as I knelt on the floor folding T-shirts and sweaters, he sat on the bed talking in Albanian on the telephone and watching me. There was always a knot of fear in my stomach and I was constantly checking and double-checking everything I did, trying to deflect his next explosion of anger. But I was most nervous of all when he was watching me, although, on this occasion, there didn't seem to be much to worry about when all I was doing was putting clothes in a suitcase. I was wrong, though, and he suddenly came flying across the room, shouting, 'Is *that* how you pack a suitcase? What kind of woman are you? How are you ever going to have a family? How could you have children and be a wife? You can't clean properly, you can't cook properly, you can't even fold clothes and pack a suitcase properly. Do you think it's all right just to push socks down the sides like that? Well, *do* you?'

It felt as though my whole body was shrinking and as I cowered away from him, I glanced up just as he reached out his hand, grabbed a fistful of my hair and pulled me to my feet, screaming at me, 'You fucking snake! How dare you look at me sideways like that with your sly, disrespectful eyes? That's the way Albanian peasants look at people. How *dare* you disrespect me? How fucking dare you?'

Then he dropped me abruptly on to the floor and as I tried to cover my head with my arms and curl my body into a protective ball, he started kicking me viciously. He was like a furious, snarling animal – and all because he didn't approve of the way I'd pushed a pair of socks into a suitcase and then looked up at him as he approached me from the side.

They say that just before people drown, they stop struggling to keep their heads above water and become almost calm, and that was how I felt at that moment. Whatever I did, however hard I tried, it seemed to make no difference and I was completely weary. *Kick me*, I thought. *Kick me as much as you want if it makes you happy* – because I knew that Kas had finally broken my spirit and I'd given up.

But, instead of kicking me again, he almost ran out of the room, and I was still lying on the floor with my eyes closed and pain radiating into every part of my body when he came back a few seconds later, carrying a gun. Dragging me up by my hair, he shoved the barrel of the gun into my mouth, crushing my lips painfully against my teeth, and said, in a quiet, cold voice that frightened me even more than his shouting, 'Never, *ever*, look at me in that way again.'

I was whimpering and terrified, although part of me wanted to shout back at him, 'Go on then, just do it. Pull the trigger. Why would I care?'

And then he took the gun out of my mouth, pushed me towards the bathroom with a force that sent me sprawling across the floor, and said, 'Now go and clean yourself up.'

Kas always told me what to wear every day, and that night he'd chosen a white mini-skirt, skimpy pink top, short zip-up jacket and shoes with stiletto heels. And by the time I was dressed and went into the living room, his mood had changed completely. Putting his hand on my shoulder, he turned me round and said, 'Look at you! You are so beautiful, woman! All the men queue up to be with you because you are so amazing. Everybody wants to know you. Let me take your photograph.'

So I stood there, confused and disorientated, while he took pictures of me and told me, 'You are my girl, my special little mouse.' And then he sat down on the sofa, pulled me on to his knee and stroked my hair as he said, 'You are my special girl and I shouldn't have done that to you. I'm sorry, but you make me so angry. If you just learned to do what I tell you and didn't disrespect me, you wouldn't ever be in trouble. But you always make mistakes.'

Again, he knocked the side of my head with his knuckles as he added, 'I don't want you to make mistakes. I want you to be a good girl, so that I don't have to be angry with you. I want you to do things properly, and then I won't have to shout at you anymore.'

I sat on his knee, crying and wishing with all my heart that I *wasn't* so stupid and that I could learn not to get things wrong all the time, while he stroked my hair again, wiped the tears from my cheeks and said, 'Ah, you're like a little dog, with your big, sad eyes. I don't want to see tears in your eyes anymore. I don't want you to cry.' I put my arms around his neck as I whispered, 'I'm sorry. I'm *so* sorry. I don't mean to be bad. I don't know why I'm so stupid or why I always make mistakes, but I *promise* I'll be better. I won't get things wrong anymore.'

Chapter 9

Although everyone kept telling my mother, 'Sophie's fine. You should just relax and be pleased she's enjoying herself,' she couldn't shake off the feeling that something was wrong. She told herself it was just because she was missing me and because it had been so out of character for me to decide not to come home in the way I'd done. But she wasn't convinced and she felt worried.

Before I'd gone to Italy, my mum had told me that if ever anything went wrong and I needed her help but couldn't speak openly on the phone for any reason, I should ask her, 'How's Auntie Linda?' One day, when I'd been in Italy for a few weeks and was talking to her on the phone, telling her for the umpteenth time that everything was fine – and then biting my lip to stop myself bursting into tears – she interrupted me and said, 'Did you want to ask about Auntie Linda?'

I knew what she meant and I wanted more than anything in the world to scream '*Yes!*' down the phone at her, but Kas was standing right beside me and although he couldn't hear what she was saying, I was terrified of making him suspicious or angry. I think, too, that I was so ashamed of what I was doing I didn't see how I would ever be able to tell my mother the truth. So I said, 'I'm okay. Stop worrying about me. Everything's fine.' I reassured her again that I was having a great time in Italy and then I said 'Goodbye', as cheerfully as I could, and handed the phone to Kas.

'What was your mother saying to you?' he asked, still holding it in his outstretched hand and watching me with his eyes narrowed. 'Why did you have to tell her not to worry?'

My heart began to thud. Perhaps he *had* heard what she'd said after all and if I didn't tell him the truth, he'd fly into a rage. But if I did tell him, I'd have to think of some plausible explanation of what she meant, and my mind was already shutting down because of the fear.

Somehow, though, I managed to keep my voice level as I said, 'Oh, it was nothing. She thought I sounded as though I had a cold and she was just asking if I was all right.' Then I shrugged and added, 'You know what mothers are like – they always worry about things like that.'

Kas continued to look at me steadily for a moment and then he said, 'Okay. But make sure you tell her you're eating properly and that everything's fine.'

In fact, I did have a cold that day. I was barely eating, standing night after night in the freezing cold and sometimes in torrential rain, and so run down that there was rarely a day when I wasn't ill in some way. But it didn't matter how ill I was, I still had to go out to work. There was just one night when Kas let me stay at home. I was exhausted and I'd had a horrible feeling all day that something really bad was going to happen if I went out. So I told him I had terrible stomach pains, and although he shouted at me, eventually he said, 'Right, stay in the bedroom and sleep. I don't want to see you looking at the television. If I see you even move, you can't imagine how much trouble you'll be in. You've cost me money, woman, and tomorrow you're going back to work, however ill you feel.' But he didn't need to warn and threaten me because I slept for almost 24 hours, and I would have stayed asleep every day and every night for a week if I'd had the chance.

Sometimes, Kas would wake me up during the day and tell me to get dressed because we were going out – usually to buy me new 'working clothes'. He always told me what to wear, and in the daytime it was tracksuit bottoms, trainers, a jacket and a cap, with my hair tied back and very little make-up, because keeping a low profile was very important to him, and his main aim was for no one to notice us.

So one day, when we were driving somewhere and I looked up just as a police car drove slowly past us, he waited until it was out of sight and then smashed my head sideways against the window.

'*Why?* Why would you look at the police?' he shouted at me. 'Are you trying to draw attention to us? Are you trying to get me into trouble? I've got fucking cocaine in this car and if I get caught, it will be your fault, and then what are you going to do? You're going to be stuck here all on your own with no one to look after you. Is that what you want?' And I felt really angry with myself for having looked at the police car without thinking about the consequences.

There were so many times when I was frightened of Kas, so many times when a knot formed in my stomach and my heart pounded in my chest as I waited for his reaction to something. One of the worst times of all was the night he decided I was cheating on him.

It was almost half past 5 on a Sunday morning, I'd been out since 8 o'clock on the Saturday night, and I was just about to start the long walk back to the flat when a car pulled up beside me. Although numb with exhaustion, I decided to go with just this one last client, but as soon as I got into his car, I realised he'd been drinking. My heart sank: drunk guys always took forever and I knew Kas would be expecting me back. And then my phone rang.

Of all the things I was frightened of – and by this time there were almost too many to count – not answering the phone when Kas rang was perhaps the most frightening of all. From the very first day, he had instilled in me the need to answer his calls immediately, and even when I did, he would threaten me and swear at me in Albanian for being so slow to respond. So it didn't matter who I was with or what I was doing, I would scrabble to reach my phone with my heart racing.

'Where are you?' Kas shouted. 'You get your arse back here – *now!*'

'I've just got into a car,' I whispered. 'It's the last one.'

'Fifteen minutes,' he said. 'You've got fifteen minutes and then I'll come looking for you.'

Fifteen minutes later, the man still hadn't finished and my phone rang again.

'Where the *fuck* are you? I'm worried sick, going out of my mind thinking something's happened to you. You could be fucking dead for all I know,' although he sounded angry rather than concerned for my safety.

'I'm coming. I'm coming,' I told him. 'It's just … I won't be long.'

Five minutes later, while the man was still grunting and fumbling and trying to focus through his drunken haze, my phone rang again.

'Woman, are you fucking with me?' Kas's voice roared in my ear. 'You see what I'm going to do to you now! I'm on my way and I'm going to fucking kill him and then I'm going to kill you. You are fucking dead, woman.'

I started trying to push the guy off me, telling him, 'You've got to go. Go! *Now!*'

'Why? What's wrong?' His speech was slurred but he must have recognised the urgency in my voice because he moved back quickly into his seat and sped off almost before I'd had time to clamber out of his car.

As I stood shivering at the side of the road, I could hear the intermittent screech of tyres as Kas's car sped down the winding hill from his flat, and when he pulled up beside me, he reached behind and flung open the back door. I bent down to get in, and he grabbed me by my hair, dragging me to the middle of the seat. Then he banged the door closed, swept the car in an arc across the road and drove with one hand on the steering wheel and the fingers of the other entwined again in my hair.

'Where *is* he?' Kas screamed. 'Where is the mother-fucker? I'm going to fucking kill him.'

I'd lost count of all the times I'd seen him in a rage, but never before had he been as furious as he was then.

'I don't know what you're talking about,' I whimpered, clutching my head with my hands to try to stop the hairs tugging painfully at my scalp.

'I know you're fucking cheating on me!' he bellowed. 'How dare you disrespect me in this way?'

'I'm not. I didn't do anything,' I sobbed. 'Please, I promise.'

'You're risking everything.' He banged my head again and again on the back of the seat until it felt as though my brain was crashing against the inside of my skull and I thought I was going to pass out. 'I could get caught by the police coming out here to look for you. I'll find him and I'll kill him. What sort of car is he driving?'

But he didn't wait for me to answer. Lifting me up by my hair, he dragged me along the seat until I was half-sitting, with my body twisted away from him, and then he started punching me, turning away occasionally to glance at the road.

By the time we arrived at the flat there was an intense, hot pain in my back and shoulders and it felt as though every muscle had been ripped apart. Kas told me to sit on the sofa and when he stood in front of me, I shut my eyes and waited for the moment when his fist would crash into my face. But, instead of hitting me, he leaned down towards me, smoothed and straightened my hair and said, in a quiet, almost normal, voice, 'Show me how much money you've got.'

I handed him the wad of notes and he sat down on the chair beside the sofa to count them. Kas always counted the money himself, sorting the notes one by one and plac-ing them in neat, orderly piles of hundreds, fifties, twenties and tens on the table in front of him, all in the same orien-tation and with their corners smoothed. He'd be angry if I'd been given any five-Euro notes – 'The money used by peasants' he called it, spitting out the words with disgust – and one night he went crazy, shouting at me and hitting me for handing him some coins. 'What sort of person pays for sex with coins?' he shrieked at me. 'And what sort of person accepts them?' So I always dreaded this moment.

On this particular night, however, although I held my breath as I always did, I'd been working for at least nine hours, so I knew there was enough money to satisfy even Kas. But suddenly he was on his feet again, screaming at me, 'You cheating bitch! How many times have I told you: do not cheat on me; do not steal from me. Do you think ...'

It was like being trapped in a horrible, illogical, never-ending dream, where nothing made sense and everything that happened was unexpected and inexplicable.

'I didn't cheat on you,' I cried. 'I didn't steal any of the money. It's all there. Everything I've earned tonight is there.'

'Don't you dare to interrupt me.' Kas spoke slowly in a voice that was cold and full of threat.

Again, I shut my eyes and held my breath, waiting for him to hit me. But this time he left the room and came back a few seconds later holding a knife in one hand and a broom in the other. I watched as he dropped the knife on to a chair and unscrewed the brush head from the broom. Then he picked up the knife again and stood, towering above me as I cowered on the sofa. In a dangerously pleas-ant voice he said, 'So. I'm going to let you choose. Which one do you want? The knife or the stick?'

'I didn't do anything wrong,' I whispered. 'Please, Kas, I ...'

'The knife or the stick?' he repeated more loudly, bend-ing down and pushing them both into my face.

'The stick,' I snivelled, and as he threw the knife on the chair and raised the stick above his head, I dropped on to the floor, locking my arms around his leg and pleading

151

with him, 'Please, *please* don't do this. I *promise* I didn't do anything. *Please* …'

The handle of the broom crashed down just once on the back of my skull and then came flying past my head as Kas threw it on the floor and shouted at me, 'Look what you've made me do now – and all because you wanted to screw someone else.'

'I didn't. I didn't do anything wrong,' I sobbed. But my voice was barely audible. Reaching out my hand to feel for the edge of the sofa, I managed to drag myself to my feet and stagger into the bathroom just in time before I was violently sick.

When I came out of the bathroom, my head was still spinning. I felt dizzy, almost as though my mind had become detached from my body and I was watching myself from the outside. And Kas was still in a fury. Grabbing me by the hair with the fingers of one hand, he yanked me towards him, and as he did so he used his other hand to punch me with such violent force that he sent my body smashing against the wall.

I was more scared of him than I'd ever been before, not least because I knew how easy it would be for him to kill me – either deliberately or inadvertently – even though I hadn't done anything wrong. And although I didn't realise what had happened until much later, that was the night he cracked my shoulder blade.

My body was already covered in bruises from all the other times he'd punched me and bashed my head repeatedly against the wall. But the pain in my neck, across my shoulders and down my arms was the worst I'd ever experienced. When he eventually waved his hand at me in disgust and told me to go to bed, I had to sleep in my clothes because I couldn't raise my arms high enough to take them off.

I was never allowed to count the money, but I did keep a rough tally in my head, so that I knew how many more customers I needed before I'd earned at least the minimum that he expected me to make every night. I'd stopped keeping the money in my boots after the first week because I was afraid of being kidnapped or of someone trying to steal it from me – and would push 50 Euros through a little hole I'd made in the lining at the back of my jacket and put the rest in a plastic bag, which I'd bury in a hole in the rough ground behind the petrol station.

One Saturday night, I worked constantly until six in the morning – at one point there were three cars lined up, all regular customers waiting for me – and I knew I must have earned a small fortune. Kas had a couple of friends staying with him, and when I got back, they were all asleep and the flat was in darkness. I hated the men being there, particularly because I knew they had no reason to care about me and that anything could happen. So I crept into the bathroom, opened the plastic bag of money, counted it and then pulled off my coat, pushing my hand through the slit in the lining and pulling frantically at the material as I searched for the notes I must have put in there and then forgotten about. And then the voice in my head shouted *No!*

I knew I must have earned at least 1,000 Euros, but however carefully I searched and however many times I counted, there was still just 600. I couldn't understand it; it simply didn't make any sense. *Think*, I told myself. *Just try to calm down and think. Where might you have hidden it? It* must *be there. There's nowhere else it can be.*

I *had* to have made a mistake in the counting. The only other alternative was that someone had stolen from me, and that seemed impossible. One thing *was* certain though – Kas was going to kill me.

I was shaking and my stomach was cramping and churning when I woke him up, whispering to him, 'I'm sorry. I'm really sorry. I've only made this tonight,' as I held out the wad of notes to show him. He got out of bed immediately and, without a word, grabbed me by the arm and pushed me ahead of him into the bathroom, locking the door behind us.

When he smiled at me, it felt as though icy-cold liquid was flooding into my heart. He sighed as he said, 'Ah! *Rrishit tim pak.* [My little grape.]' But then he snatched the notes from my hand and counted them and his voice was hard and pitiless as he hissed at me, 'Do you think you can come home at 6 o'clock in the morning with just this? Just wait until my friends leave. We will deal with this later. And while you wait, you'd better think, woman. Think where my money has gone. I know you've cheated on me and stolen from me, and I want to know what you've done with my money.'

'I *haven't*. I promise I haven't,' I stammered. 'The only thing that could have happened is that someone's taken some of the money I buried. I ...'

'*Why?*' he snapped, twisting my arm until I thought it would break. 'Why would someone take *some* of the money? Are you stupid? Do you think everyone else is as stupid as you are? If someone was going to rob you, they'd take it *all*. Do you think they thought they'd stumbled on a bank, so they decided to take some now and come back for the rest when they needed it? Is that what you think? Don't you dare lie to me, woman. Just see what I will do to you when you steal from me.'

I didn't sleep at all that night. Instead, I lay awake, crying silently into my pillow, dreading what I knew was coming and wondering what my mother was doing and what she'd think if she knew the kind of life I was really leading.

The next day, as soon as his friends had gone, Kas slapped me across the face, shrugged his shoulders and said, 'What you lost, you can make up today.' Then he switched on the television, lit a cigarette and turned his back on me.

His unpredictability was as unnerving as his temper because it meant that I never knew what he was going to do – and I sometimes wondered whether he did either.

For seven nights every week it often felt as though I was going round and round in a revolving door. I'd stand at the side of the road, a car would pull up, the man would ask how much, I'd get in the car and we'd drive to the track beside the petrol station, then afterwards he'd drop me off, another car would pull up …

The nights had been cold right from the start, but the temperature dropped steadily as the weeks went by, until even if it was warm and sunny during the day, it was so cold once the sun went down that however many layers of jumpers and jackets I wore, I was always freezing. It didn't help that my weight had dropped to about 6½ stone and I was smoking up to 20 cigarettes a night, although I'd rarely have a chance to smoke one before the next car pulled up beside me. In England, I'd hardly ever smoked, and the fact that I did so now seemed to be just another indication that Sophie was disappearing. Perhaps because of my lack of appetite, loss of weight and a persistent cough – which the cigarettes and standing in the cold did nothing to improve – I seemed to be getting significantly weaker almost by the day. So sometimes it was a relief to be in a warm car for 15 minutes, particularly when I was with one of the men who were nice to me. One night, when it was so cold it felt as though ice crystals were forming in my bones, my teeth were chattering so violently that when a car pulled up beside me and the man asked 'How much?', he could hardly understand what I was saying when I told him the price. I was so grateful to get into the warmth for a few minutes that I didn't look at him properly until I was sitting beside him in the car, and just as I realised that he was as high as

a kite on drugs, drunk or completely crazy – or all three –
he locked the doors.

'Let me out of the car,' I told him, struggling to keep my
voice level so that he wouldn't know how panic-stricken I
really was. 'Open the door. I want to go.'

But he'd already pulled across the road into the traffic
and when he reached towards me with one hand I thought
for a horrible moment that he was going to open the door
and push me out. Instead, though, he grabbed me by the
throat and said, 'No. Come. Come with me. It's okay.'

Just stay calm, I told myself. *Don't struggle. It'll be fine.*

Although he loosened his grip, he kept his hand on my
throat as he drove and then stopped the car in an alleyway
a short distance along the main road.

'Let me out,' I demanded angrily again. 'Open the door.
Vai via! No scopare.'

And, suddenly, both his hands were around my throat,
his fingernails digging into my neck, and he was screaming into my face in Italian. I tried to push him away and
shouted back at him, '*Vai via!* Go!' But I could barely
breathe and the words came out in a strangled croak.
'*Mio ragazzo è albanese*,' I stuttered. But he just laughed
as he said, '*Dove è il vostro denaro?* Your money – where
is it?'

I didn't have much money with me at the time – most
of that night's earnings were buried in the soil behind the
petrol station – and my first instinct was to give him what
I had. But I knew that even if I gave him money, there was

nothing to stop him killing me – and if he didn't, Kas probably would when I arrived home again without the full amount.

When I'd realised earlier that he'd locked the doors of the car, I'd slipped my hand into my pocket and curled my fingers around my phone. Now I began to press Kas's number. I waited a few seconds to give him time to answer and then pulled the phone out of my pocket and shouted into it, 'You've got to come. The alleyway by the dead tree. He's a psychopath.' The man reached out to try to knock the phone out of my hand, but I snatched it away, so he grabbed me around the throat again and started banging my head against the headrest.

I don't know where Kas was when he got my phone call, but it seemed to be only seconds later that his car came screeching into the alleyway behind us and, before the man had a chance to react, Kas was thumping with his fists on the window beside him. Still startled and bemused, the guy turned to look at Kas and I reached across and unlocked the doors. Immediately, the driver's door flew open and Kas dragged the man out of his seat and started kicking him. Then he pushed him, face-down, on to the bonnet of the car and punched him repeatedly on the back of his head so that his face smashed again and again on to the metal and I was certain Kas was going to kill him.

There was blood pouring from the man's face when Kas eventually lifted him up by the scruff of his neck, pulling him to his feet and half-dragging, half-carrying him around the car to where I was standing, frozen to the spot by cold and fear.

'Now tell her you're sorry,' Kas shouted, his fingers clamping on to the man's jaw as he forced him to look at me.

'I'm sorry. I'm sorry,' the guy mumbled.

'Now fuck off. *Go!*' Kas released his grip on him abruptly and the man stumbled back around his car and threw himself into the driver's seat. Then he locked the doors, started the engine and swerved sharply around Kas's car as he pulled out on to the main road.

I sat in the car beside Kas, waiting for the tirade of verbal abuse and the physical assault I knew was coming, but he just patted my knee and said, 'Well done. You did the right thing – you didn't show him that you were frightened. You did really well.' And suddenly I felt as though the ordeal I'd just been through had been worth it for the reward of knowing that, for once, I'd got something right and Kas was pleased with me.

One of my main concerns as I stood on the street every night was trying to dodge the *Carabinieri*, who were always on the lookout for me. Sometimes, I'd see them coming and I'd have time to hide in the trees behind the petrol station. But often they'd pull up beside me before I could get away and tell me, 'You can't stay here. *Go!*' So I'd walk along the road for a few minutes, waiting for them to drive away, and then go back to my spot.

On the nights when they picked me up and took me to the police station, they'd keep me there until about 5 o'clock in the morning and then let me go. In fact, once I'd got over my initial humiliation at being picked up by the police at all, it wasn't such a bad thing – at least it meant I could spend the night inside in the warmth and then have a good excuse to give Kas for not having earned any money. And the *Carabinieri* were usually all right with me.

So although I was always annoyed with myself for having been stupid enough to get caught, I wasn't actually worried when a police car pulled in beside me one night and I was told, 'Not tonight. Get in the car. You have to come with us.'

This time, though, when we arrived at the police station, the two policemen started to ask me questions, insisting that they didn't believe my story about being South African and demanding to know where I really came from, until eventually it seemed pointless to keep up the pretence.

'Were you doing this in England?' one of the policemen asked me. 'What is your address there?'

For a moment, I thought about telling them, 'I'm not what you think I am. I'm not Jenna. My name is Sophie and I don't do things like this. I had a good job in England and I've got a mum and a family and they love me.' But there was no point. Even if they believed me, even if they hadn't been sent by Kas to find out if I'd break under pressure and give him away, they couldn't really help me because eventually he would know what I'd done and he'd hurt my family and then kill me.

So I gave them the alternative story Kas had told me to tell – that I'd been a pole dancer in England and had come to Italy to earn better money – and eventually they shrugged and said I could leave. But it was only midnight, I was tired and there was a small part of me that wanted to fight back against Kas for the way he treated me and for always being so worried about protecting himself and so indifferent to what might happen to me. Whenever I was picked up and asked where I lived, I had to give an address in the city. So I asked the policemen, 'Can I wait here until I can catch a train back to town? I was supposed to meet someone, but it's too late now.' And they shrugged again and let me stay in the warmth of the reception area.

So I sat there for the rest of the night, praying Kas wouldn't drive past and see me through the window, and then, at 5 o'clock in the morning, I walked home and told Kas that the police had kept me at the station. And although I was terrified in case he ever discovered the truth, the fear was almost worth it for the sense that, for once, I hadn't been completely under his control.

One night not long afterwards, a people-carrier pulled off the road beside me and I bent down beside the open passenger window. Normally, I only ever approached cars on the driver's side, but it had stopped at an odd angle, and it was only as I looked in through the window that I realised that although the car was unmarked, the guy was wearing the uniform of the *Guardia di Finanza*, the police force that deals with smuggling and drugs. I took a step backwards and then froze as he pointed a gun directly into my face and shouted, '*Vai! Vai! Vai! Vai via!*'

I knew my life meant nothing to many of the men who stopped their cars on the road beside me at night, and less than nothing to most of the policemen, who saw me not as a person but as a low-life irritation. And I knew, too, that there was nothing to stop this man shooting me if he wanted to.

I ran behind the car, but he'd already opened the door and jumped out, and when I stumbled, he stood over me, pointing his gun into my face again and shouting at me to go away. The temptation to run was almost overwhelming, but I forced myself not to because I was afraid he might shoot me in the back and then make up some story about what had happened, which no one would ever bother to question. So I got to my feet and began to back away slowly from the car. And then suddenly, for no obvious reason, he lowered the gun, got back behind the wheel and drove away.

I was shaking violently and my mind was so numbed by shock that for a moment I couldn't remember Kas's number, and all I could do when he answered the phone was keep repeating the words, 'Oh my God'. Eventually, though, I managed to calm down enough to tell him, 'Someone's just pulled a gun on me.'

'Stay there,' Kas told me, and I was sobbing as I walked to the back of the petrol station and crouched down on the grass behind the low wall separating it from the patch of woodland to wait for him.

A few minutes later, as I sat beside Kas in his car, he asked me, 'What was the number plate?' and I tried to remember.

'I think it had a two in it,' I told him. 'Or … Or it might have been a three. I can't remember. I was so scared.'

Instantly he was angry and shouting at me, 'How many times have I told you always memorise the number plate? Can't you even do that one simple thing? You're wasting my time, and what if someone saw me coming here to pick you up? Do you want to get me into trouble? What if he comes again, on another night? What if he ends up shooting you dead? Then what do I do? How am I going to know what's happened to you if you don't know the registration number of his car?' For some reason, though, there was little force behind his single punch and he never mentioned the incident again.

So, once again, I was left feeling confused and bemused about what made Kas angry and wondering whether the policeman who'd just threatened to shoot me was actually one of his friends whom he'd sent to make sure I never forgot to be afraid.

Chapter 10

After a while I became quite good at identifying different nationalities – by physical features, such as the shape of their head, as well as the way they spoke Italian. Some of them were angry when I told them I could only go with Italians, and I didn't dare say why. Luckily, few of them asked for reasons, and most would just swear at me and spin the wheels of their cars as they pulled out into the traffic again. But I didn't always get it right, and after I told one man 'No Moroccans', despite his insistence that he was Italian, he came back a couple of nights later with his identity card!

Sometimes, though, I didn't pay careful enough attention until it was almost too late and one night it was only as I was just about to get into a car that I noticed the guy looked Macedonian. When I asked him, he said he was Italian, but the music playing on his car stereo was definitely Eastern European and so I told him 'No'. I was expecting him to swear at me, but my heart almost stopped beating when he leapt out of his car and went completely crazy, shouting at me and waving his hands in my face.

I knew I mustn't let him see my fear, so I shouted back at him and told him he'd better go, because my boyfriend was Albanian. As I said the words, a car turned off the main road and pulled in beside his, and when we both looked towards it, I almost burst into tears of relief when I saw that it was Kas. Pretending not to know me, he leaned out of the window and asked 'How much?' and I edged away from the guy as I told him a price. 'Okay. *Andiamo*,' Kas said, opening the passenger-side door, and I jumped into his car and we sped away.

He dropped me off further down the road and told me to walk back to 'my spot' while he followed the man to make sure he didn't return. I felt a rush of gratitude to him for being there when I needed someone, but at the same time I felt uneasy because I couldn't help wondering how he'd just happened to turn up when he did. Was it chance that he'd been close by, or did he often watch me when I didn't know he was there, to make sure I was doing what I was supposed to be doing?

It was just another uncertainty among all the doubts and insecurities I was living with. There seemed to be no one I could trust and nothing I could rely on – even Kas's anger. It was impossible to guess at his reaction to anything. He seemed to have a split personality, although he was 10 different people rather than just two. Sometimes he'd drive past the petrol station and wave to me, or even open his car window and shout 'I love you', and one night he beeped his horn and threw me a rose. Most of the time, however, he was either in a rage or on the verge of one, and his sudden violent outbursts and loss of control were often triggered by something completely trivial or imagined.

One night, when I hadn't made enough money, he went from angry to crazy within just a fraction of a second, hurling his mobile phone across the room at me so that it smashed against the wall and sent out an explosion of plastic splinters. 'You've got five seconds,' he shouted. 'Just five seconds to clear that up.' I began to scrabble around on the floor, making little moaning, whimpering noises as I searched under the furniture for bits of debris. But I was so shocked and frightened that my hands were clumsy and as I fumbled, dropping the fragments I'd already picked up, Kas started to count, slowly, 'One. Two …'

At that moment, his other phone rang and he walked into the bedroom to answer it. I could hear him pacing backwards and forwards across the bedroom floor, and every so often I heard snatches of what he was saying. Although he was speaking in Albanian, I realised he was talking to his mother. Then he shouted the word 'schizo-phrenia' and it sounded as though he'd kicked a chair against the bedroom door. But when he came back into the living room a few minutes later, his anger had completely evaporated and he spoke calmly as he told me, 'I'm sorry. I've told my mother what happened tonight and she says that I mustn't hurt you anymore.'

I didn't know if it was true, and, if not, what else might have caused his abrupt change of mood. He'd told me before that his mother wanted us to get married – although that seemed very unlikely, not least because she'd never even met me. And it wasn't the first time I'd wondered whether it might not be Kas who ran his own operation after all.

One day, when he was in one of his rare good moods, he told me he'd fallen in love with me the first time he saw me.

'How can you love me?' I asked him. 'What is there to love about me? Look at me. I'm like a zombie – I don't speak except when I'm spoken to; I only smile when you tell me to smile. How can you say you love someone like that?'

But he just laughed and said, 'You're crazy, woman. This is all in your head.'

And, for a moment, I wondered if perhaps he really *did* love me and I just couldn't see it because I was so used to believing I was unlovable. I'd wanted for as long as I could remember to be swept off my feet by someone who would take charge of everything and create an amazing life for us to live together. The problem was that whenever anyone told me they loved me, I'd always push them away – or let them down, like I'd let Erion down. It was as though I couldn't help myself. I simply didn't believe them. In my mind, they were either lying or mistaken. Because how could someone whose own father doesn't even like her be worthy of anyone's love? So I was already confused and bewildered even before Kas made me unsure about almost everything.

It sounds strange, I know, when, after everything he'd done and the way he treated me, I say that I wondered if Kas loved me, and it's difficult to describe how I felt. Although I hated him, I wanted to believe that there was some explanation I could understand for what he was doing to me. And the only explanation that seemed to make any sense at the time was that it was somehow all my fault.

Kas and I had been friends and had talked regularly on the phone for four years before I'd arrived in Italy, so he knew almost as much about my fears, anxieties and psychological hang-ups as I knew myself – or perhaps even more. And he was clever enough to be able to use what he knew to his advantage. Put simplistically, perhaps the fact that he frightened and bullied me and criticised everything I did, just like my father had done throughout my child-hood, meant that I wanted him to love me – in the same way that I'd always wanted my father to do.

One evening, when he was about to drop me off at the bottom of the hill, he suddenly said, 'Oh my God, you're like an angel. I get goose bumps when I look at you. You drive me crazy. I can't control myself when I see you.'

Immediately I was wary, uncertain whether he was serious or his words were sarcastic and the prelude to an eruption of anger, because sometimes he appeared to be saying something nice to me when actually he was about to criticise and shout at me. This time, though, his good humour seemed to be genuine and he drove along the main road, turned the car on to a lane, told me to take off my leggings and had sex with me. He didn't use a condom and I was so pathetically grateful for those few minutes when he was being nice to me that it didn't even cross my mind to ask him to – not that I'd have dared to do so anyway.

Sex with Kas didn't occur very often, but when it did it was just like having sex with all the other men – there was no emotion involved; it was just something that was being done to me. Sometimes, he'd wake me up in the morning by calling 'Come and give me a hug and a kiss' and I'd get out of bed instantly – even when I was asleep, there must have been part of my mind that was alert and ready to respond to anything he told me to do – and would pad across the bedroom floor and into the living room to lie with him on the sofa.

One day he hugged me and stroked my hair as he told me, 'You know I'll always look after you, don't you, little mouse? I've never cared for anyone the way I care about you. I'm sorry you have to do the things you have to do, but you won't have to do them forever. One day we'll go travelling. We'll be able to go wherever we want and do whatever we want to do.' But although I was grateful because he was being nice to me, I knew he was lying and that it would never be over. Whatever I did would never be enough, because Kas would always want more money.

Moments like that were rare, though, and although at one time I might have been beguiled by the thought of sharing a life with Kas, it now just filled me with dread. But I put my arms around him and clung to him like a child, focusing on the pleasure of being comforted and on the relief I felt because, for a while at least, he wasn't being crazy.

He never let me spend the whole night with him and sometimes I'd ask, 'Why are you so mean to me? I'm never allowed to come to you; I have to wait until you give me permission. Why won't you let me get near you?' And, if he was in a good mood, he'd say, 'Sometimes it's just not right and you need to learn that you have to wait. You can't have things simply because you want them.' So I *would* wait – like a little dog – trying not to get things wrong and trying to be good enough to be worthy of his notice.

One night before I went out to work, he told me to iron his shirt. I hated having to do things like that because I was so nervous and so afraid of making a mistake that, however hard I tried not to, I'd always end up making one. But, to my relief, this time he barely glanced at me while I was ironing and he put the warm shirt on without comment.

Later, when he was dressed and smelling strongly of aftershave, he stood in the kitchen doorway and said, 'Look at me! What a beauty! Everyone's going to want to talk to me tonight. Do you wonder where I'm going? Go on, why don't you ask me? I know what you're thinking. You're thinking, *It isn't fair that he's out having fun while I'm working.* But that's just the way things are. I do what I have to do – I go out and see people and take care of my business – and you do what you have to do. It's the way it is, that's all.'

Yes, it is unfair, I thought. *You're absolutely fine. And while you're out having a good time, I'll be having sex with men I don't know, who may or may not pay me and who may or may not let me get out of their cars unhurt.* But I said nothing, because I'd learned not to react in any way. This time, though, even saying nothing turned out to be wrong, and he suddenly turned on me, shouting, 'So you're happy with this arrangement, are you? You think this is okay? Obviously you don't want to know where I'm going because you don't care about me.'

Sometimes, when Kas was in a good mood, I'd describe to him some of the men I'd been with, and one day he asked me, 'Do you ever enjoy it? Tell me the truth.' He said it with a smile and when I was shocked and said '*No!*', he laughed and kept insisting, 'Go on, you can tell me. Surely there must have been times when you enjoyed it.'

'No, never,' I said again.

'You're lying!' he retorted, but he was still laughing. 'You're expecting me to believe that you have sex at least 20 times every night and you've never once enjoyed it?'

'No, I haven't,' I told him, and I wondered how he could be so completely mistaken about what it was like to be forced to have sex with strangers. But I knew that his questions were leading *some*where, and as the hairs on the back of my neck stood up, I was instantly alert.

It seemed that, for whatever reason, he was determined not to let the matter drop. He kept asking me over and over again, and then he said, 'Come on. You can tell me the truth. There must have been one. Of all those men, there must have been one who was different. Who was he?' And eventually I decided to lie, just to make him stop his relentless probing, and I said, 'Okay, there *was* just one time.'

It was as though a switch had been flipped in his brain. The smile disappeared from his face and he launched himself across the room at me, grabbing me by the hair and yanking my head back sharply as he shouted, 'You fucking bitch. How weak are you? How fucking *dare* you disrespect me? You're a disgrace. You're disgusting.' And even though I'd lied, I knew that he was right, not because I enjoyed having sex with strangers – I didn't, ever – but because of what he was making me do.

One night, I was with quite an old, nice guy I'd been with a few times before when Kas rang. There were rules about answering the phone – as there were about everything: I was only allowed to answer calls from Kas's number, and I had to answer after no more than three rings. This time, however, I didn't get to my phone before he rang off, and although I called him back immediately, it was too late.

'What the fuck are you doing?' he shrieked. 'How dare you not answer the phone when I call you? You, woman, you wait till I get hold of you.' And then he described in graphic detail what he would do to me, while the man I was with sat beside me in open-mouthed amazement, not able to make out what Kas was actually saying, but clearly shocked by the angry, shrieking voice he could hear.

When Kas finally rang off, I tried to pretend everything was all right, although in reality I was shaking and close to panic. The guy could obviously see that I was upset because he smiled, patted my hand and said, 'Let's just get out of here. Let's go somewhere else.'

Kas told me repeatedly that I was never to go anywhere other than my usual places without telling him first, but suddenly I felt exhausted. I was weary of trying to remember all the things I was supposed to do and not do and, what the hell, I was in trouble anyway. So I tried to smile too as I said, 'Okay, let's just go.'

We hadn't driven far along the main road when I glanced in the wing mirror and saw Kas's car right behind us. My instinct was to turn my head, but even though I didn't, and I kept staring straight ahead, Kas sent me a text message saying, 'Don't pretend you haven't seen me. You're cheating on me, aren't you?'

It was ridiculous and I didn't respond to it, or say anything to the man I was with, and after a while Kas stopped following us and I spent the rest of the night dreading the punishment I knew lay in store for me when I got back to the flat.

The man I was with was at least 40 years older than me, and the only reason I was with him at all was because I was earning money for Kas. I didn't want to be there. I didn't want to be with that guy or any other; I didn't want to be with Kas, and I didn't want to be in Italy. I wanted to be at home with my family, doing normal things – sitting on the sofa between my mother and my sister watching television, or playing a computer game with my little brothers, or talking on the phone to a friend while I sat in a café during my lunch break from work, making arrangements for what we were going to do at the weekend. In fact, I wanted to be doing those things so badly I didn't know how much longer I could go on living the way Kas was making me live.

Surprisingly perhaps, I didn't ever consider taking my own life. In fact, I was so afraid that Kas – or someone who'd picked me up on the street – was going to kill me that keeping myself alive became almost a fixation. Every single night when I was in Italy, I would stand at the side of the road, press the palms of my hands together until my wrists ached and say the same words in my head: 'Please God, don't let anything happen to me. Please God, keep me safe.' Then I'd look up at the moon and imagine my mother looking at it too, and for that moment I'd feel I was close to her. I'd tell myself all I had to do was believe that one day I was going to escape and be with her again, and then everything would be all right.

On another night, a man gave me 150 Euros to go back to his house with him for an hour. I was rake thin and, although I didn't realise it at the time, I looked like a child – and maybe, creepily, that was part of my appeal to some of the men. But this man just seemed lonely and he was kind to me. He took me into his small, warm kitchen, told me to sit down at the table and made me the best omelette I've ever tasted in my life. Then he handed me a mug of steaming hot coffee and urged me, 'Eat! Drink! You look so cold. This will warm you up.' When I'd eaten, he showed me pictures of his family and I tried not to cry, and afterwards he put handfuls of sweets in my pockets, as if I really were a child, and then he dropped me off near the petrol station, patted my shoulder like a benevolent uncle and said '*Stai attenta.* [Be careful.]'

I had one regular customer who was really good-looking, although very shy, and despite the fact that he didn't speak much English, he always wanted to talk to me. He used to bring a blanket to put on the seat of the car and every time he dropped me back at my spot afterwards, he'd say, 'God bless. I will pray for you.' One night when he came, he told me his mother had found a condom wrapper in the car and that she'd been very angry with him. I laughed, because he must have been at least 30, but I felt sad, too, because I missed *my* mother desperately.

Every night before I went out, I'd stand in the bathroom and whisper, 'Please, *please*, don't let anything happen to me tonight,' and as I waited at the side of the road for customers, I'd look up at the sky and think, *Mum is out there somewhere and she can see the same stars and the same moon.* And although it was a comforting thought in some ways, because it made me feel closer to her, I couldn't bear to think that despite the fact we could be looking at the same sky at exactly the same moment, we might just as well be in completely different worlds. In my heart, I've always felt that no matter how bad things get, I'll be okay; something will happen to make everything all right again. And on all those nights in Italy, I *had* to believe that was true, but I'd never imagined it was possible to feel so lost and so alone.

The way my father had treated me and the rest of my family had made me unwilling – if not unable – to trust anyone, and it had taken me a long time after I'd first met Kas to accept his friendship. And now he'd destroyed my trust completely. But maybe, however bad our experiences, we never give up hope of finding someone we can confide in, because there *was* one guy to whom I came close to telling the truth. He was in the *Polizia* – yet another of the Italian police forces – and the first time I saw him he was in a police car with a colleague and he asked me what my name was.

'Jenna,' I told him.

'No, I want to know your *real* name,' he said, and he smiled at me.

'I've told you, it's Jenna.' I felt in my pocket for a cigarette, looking away from him as I lit it to try to hide my discomfort.

'It's okay. You're not in any trouble,' he laughed. 'I just want to know what you're really called.'

And, for some reason, I told him.

'Ah So*ffee*a,' he said, and it sounded so much nicer than Sophie that I didn't correct him.

'*Alora*, So*ffee*a, are you okay?' he asked, and when I assured him that I was, he smiled again and called '*Ciao*' as they drove away.

He came back a couple of nights later, but this time he was on his own and driving a BMW. I didn't recognise him until I bent down to look in through the window and he said, cheerfully, '*Ciao*, So*ffee*a. *Come stai? Tutta bene?* [How are you? Is everything okay?]'

'*La Polizia?*' I asked him.

'*Si, si. Andiamo.* Let's go,' he said, reaching across to open the passenger door.

When I got into the car, he told me, 'My name is Angelo,' and I suddenly had an overwhelming feeling of sadness because I knew that, in another life, he might be someone who could have been my boyfriend, but I was so completely separated from that life that there was no way I could ever cross over to it from the twilight zone in which I was living.

Angelo was gorgeous, as well as very sweet. He didn't want sex; he just wanted to talk. I felt comfortable with

177

him and I really wanted to be able to trust him, but I knew I couldn't risk it. I kept asking him, 'Who are you really? Are you trying to trick me? Why have you come here just to talk to me?' And he told me that when he'd come last time, with his colleague, he'd seen something in my eyes that made him sad and he'd decided he wanted to get to know me.

He came again a few nights later, and again we just talked. And then, the next time, he said he wanted to take me back to his house. 'Here, take this,' he said, trying to drop a wad of Euros into my hands. I pushed it away and told him it would feel wrong to take his money, but he insisted – maybe because he suspected I'd get into trouble if I didn't take it – and eventually I accepted it.

Angelo was the only guy with whom it had ever felt as though it was more than just 'having sex', and when I'd been to his house with him a few times, he said, 'Come and be with me.' He asked how much I thought a policeman would earn in England and talked about us living there together, and for just one brief moment I allowed myself to believe that running away with him might actually be possible. When he asked again for my phone number, though, I told him I couldn't give it to him.

'Well then, at least take mine,' he said. But I was too frightened in case Kas found out. And at that moment my phone rang and Kas asked 'Where are you?'

'I'm on my way,' I told him, hoping he couldn't hear the guilt in my voice.

'What's the matter?' he snapped immediately. 'Why do you sound strange? Where have you been?' And then, speaking more quietly, he asked, 'Are you with the *flic* [cops]?'

I'd been desperately trying to think of something to tell him, but my mind had frozen and I almost cried with relief at being given this way out.

'Yes. Yes, that's right,' I told him.

'Working?' he asked.

'Yes.'

'Okay. Well, you should have fucking told me. The phone could be bugged and I could have been recorded by now.' And, abruptly, the line went dead.

Angelo was watching me and as I put the phone back in my pocket he asked, 'Is everything okay?'

'Yes,' I answered, trying to smile. 'It's just a friend, making sure I can get home.'

He tried again to make me take his phone number, and again I refused, although there were many times later when I wished I hadn't and that I'd asked Angelo for his help, because I *really* liked him and I know he would have helped me. But, because of Kas's erratic, violent behaviour, I'd lost any confidence I'd ever had in my own judgement, as well as the ability to think things through clearly, and I didn't dare trust Angelo. Instead, I turned away from him so that I didn't have to see the hurt in his eyes, and I never saw him again.

One night when a customer dropped me off, there was a dark-haired girl standing in my spot. Although I knew

179

other girls sometimes worked further down the road and on some of the surrounding streets, no one had ever come near my spot before and I was surprised by how territorial I felt.

'Excuse me, but this is my place,' I told her firmly, in good enough Italian for her to understand me. But she just waved her arms and made a little run at me, shouting 'No, no, no', and that was when I noticed how hard she looked.

My immediate instinct was to scuttle away because I knew that some of the girls who worked in the area had a reputation for being quite crazy, and the last thing I wanted was to get into an argument with one of them. But then I heard Kas's voice in my head saying, 'Fear is weakness, and as soon as someone sees it in you, you've lost.' So I clenched my fists to stop my hands shaking and told her again she'd have to go. And again she shouted at me and stood her ground.

I didn't want to go round to the back of the petrol station in case she cornered me there. So, watching her carefully, I walked a few metres further along the road to phone Kas and, just minutes later, his car turned on to the dirt track.

Yeah, well, now we'll see who has to move on, I thought, triumphantly. To my astonishment, however, Kas greeted the girl in Albanian and chatted to her for a while before telling me, 'It's okay. She's my friend's girl. I'm going to take her down the road and put her somewhere else.'

She pushed me out of the way as she walked around his car to the passenger door and then smirked at me as she got in, and I was annoyed because she seemed to think she'd somehow 'won'. And then I realised that I saw her as a rival – which meant I'd accepted, on some level at least, that I was a prostitute and this was my life, and suddenly I felt very miserable and very frightened.

Over the next few weeks, several things happened that made me increasingly nervous and I began to have a sense of foreboding. Perhaps it was just because what I was doing was dangerous – in many ways – and so it seemed likely that the longer I did it, the more often I was tempting fate and eventually I was going to get hurt.

There was one man who'd come a couple of times and who I didn't like, and my heart sank when his car pulled up beside me again one night. I didn't know why he made me feel so uncomfortable; there was just something creepy about him I couldn't identify, and I'd found that the best way of dealing with it was to make my mind go blank when I was with him. Later, as he was driving me back to the petrol station and I was breathing a sigh of relief because it was over, the darkness was suddenly lit by blue flashing lights and I could see that the whole place was swarming with *Carabinieri*, their cars blocking off both entrances to the dirt track.

'Don't stop,' I told the man. 'There's somewhere else you can drop me off.' I began to direct him to the place I'd worked with Cara on my first couple of nights, but when I told him 'Turn left here', he drove straight past the turning. '*Left!*' I said again. 'You've missed it. We have to go back.'

And then I looked at him and it was clear from the expression on his face that he hadn't made a mistake; he was ignoring me.

One of the most important of Kas's many rules was that I was never to let a man take me somewhere I didn't know. 'You must always be the one who gives directions,' he told me. 'You must say where to stop and where he must drop you off afterwards.' I knew that not knowing where I was meant I couldn't phone Kas for help, which meant that if some man decided to kill me and dump my body, it might not be found for weeks or months, or maybe ever.

A few seconds later, the man turned his car off the road onto a track I didn't know and demanded that I had sex with him again. I tried not to sound frightened when I refused, but I'm small and at the time weighed just 6½ stone, so I was no match for a heavily built, six-foot man – although at least, despite being scary and creepy, he hadn't previously shown any signs of being violent or aggressive.

While we were having sex, I tried to think what I could do if he turned on me afterwards – and I tried to close my mind to the thought that whatever happened was actually completely out of my hands. So I was astounded when he gave me some more money, started the engine of his car and drove back onto the main road. But then, as he was driving, he opened his trousers, took hold of my hand and told me to touch him. When I snatched my hand away, he reached for it again, and said, patiently, 'Do you want me to drop you off somewhere else? If you want me to do this favour for you, then you must do a favour for me.' And I knew I had no choice.

I avoided the *Carabinieri* that night, but there was one policeman who was determined to move me on and get rid of me. His name was Roberto Rossi and he was the chief of the local police – a large, angry, aggressive man whose absolute hatred of me was one of the reasons I began to feel as though trouble was brewing for me. He seemed to have decided to make it his mission in life to harass me so that it was impossible for me to work in the area, and there were several nights when his car screeched to a halt beside me and he jumped out, stood directly in front of me and sprayed my face with saliva as he shouted, '*No scopare! Vai via!*'

I'd turn and walk away down the road and he'd jump back in his car and drive slowly behind me, illuminating me in his headlights for all the world to see. If I ran and tried to hide, he always found me, and as I couldn't go home while he was following me, I'd just have to keep walking, praying he'd tire of the game or would be called away to a crime more worthy of his high-ranking attention.

On some nights, if there were a lot of police in the area for some reason, I'd go to another spot. It was about 15 minutes' walk away from my usual place and on a busy main road, with only short stretches of pavement and very few streetlights. Sometimes, I'd get locked into a ridiculous, exhausting game of cat and mouse with Rossi, dodging from one spot to the other while he drove backwards and forwards along the road looking for me. And then, one night, he stopped his car beside me, smiled a nasty, spiteful smile and handed me a piece of paper – a Persona non Grata notice that banned me from the region for seven days.

He waved his hands at me and told me to go, and as I walked along the main road, he followed me in his car, as he often did. This time though, he shone a huge, powerful spotlight on me and, speaking through a megaphone in a loud, insistent monotone, kept repeating the words, '*Vai via! Andiamo. Vai via!*' Every car that passed slowed down to have a good look at the girl who was scuttling along the edge of the road under a spotlight, and I felt so humiliated that I wished the ground would open under my feet.

At one point, I got quite far ahead of Rossi's car and when it stopped for a moment, I began to run, holding out my hand to hitchhike. It was only a minute or two before a car pulled up beside me and I jumped in without even looking at the driver, shouting, 'Go! *Go!*' Luckily, the man wasn't a serial killer or a deranged kidnapper, and he dropped me off at another spot, where I spent the rest of the night being picked up by customers and hiding from Rossi.

All night, I dreaded the prospect of having to tell Kas about the eviction notice. I knew I had to though, because it meant I wouldn't be able to go out on the streets and work for seven days. I was terrified as I handed it to him and, while he read it, I stood with my head bent and my hands clasped so tightly together that my fingers began to go numb.

But when Kas eventually looked up at me again, he just shrugged and said, 'So?'

'Well, I can't go back there,' I told him. 'If he catches me, I'll be put in prison.'

'So don't let him catch you.' Kas screwed the piece of paper into a ball and tossed it on to the table beside him.

For a moment, I felt angry. He was forever flying into rages with me because he professed to think I'd done something that might result in him going to prison. But it was clear that he couldn't care less about me and that as long as I didn't implicate him, he wouldn't lose a moment's sleep if *I* was put in prison – or ended up lying dead in the dirt somewhere.

To Kas, though, the subject was closed, and I knew better than to try to keep it open. I had no alternative other than to carry on working and dodging the police.

Not long after my night in the spotlight, I saw the two Albanian guys whose car Kas had shot at. I was standing at the side of the road waiting for customers when they drove past, very slowly, staring at me. I was already a bundle of nerves – every sound made me jump – and I suddenly felt exposed and very vulnerable. And as the hairs on the back of my neck stood up, I had a sense of impending doom.

So when Kas told me a few days later that we were going to France, I could have cried with relief. He didn't tell me any details and, of course, I didn't ask any questions. He just woke me up earlier than usual a couple of days after he'd mentioned it and said, 'Pack a bag before you go out tonight. We're going to drive through the night to France when you've finished work. You'll need to get some sleep in the car because you'll be going straight out again when we get there.'

I'd been in Italy for about four months and although I was very happy to be leaving, I dreaded the thought of having to start all over again in a place I didn't know, where I wouldn't even have my regular customers to check up on me from time to time and ask if I was all right. But at least I spoke a bit of French, so maybe I wouldn't feel quite as lost and frightened as I'd done when I started working in Italy.

The *Carabinieri* followed me everywhere that night. It didn't seem to matter where I went, I couldn't get rid of them. They watched every move I made and I began to wonder how I was ever going to get home. In the end, I sat on a park bench and smoked one cigarette after another while I waited for them to get bored and leave me alone. It meant I didn't earn much that night, but I felt as though I'd dodged a bullet and I couldn't wait to be on the road to France.

I finished earlier than usual, and back at the flat Kas sat on the bed making phone calls while I packed the last few things into a suitcase. Suddenly, he threw his phone across the room and shouted at me, 'Are you stupid, woman?' I was kneeling on the floor beside the case and as I toppled over backwards, he stood up and grabbed hold of my T-shirt, twisting the material in his fingers and picking me up like a rag doll. Then he flung me against the wall and held me there, shaking me and slapping my face as he bellowed, 'Can you still not pack a suitcase properly, woman? Have I not told you this before? Did I not explain it to you in a way that even someone as stupid as you are could understand?'

He dropped me on the floor and began pulling everything out of the case. Somewhere inside me a tiny flame of resentment flickered for a moment and I thought, *I am not a child. I do not need to be told how to pack clothes in a suitcase.* Clearly, though, Kas thought otherwise, and he slapped my face again, snatched up a T-shirt and, as he began to fold it, said, '*This* is how you fold clothes. *This* is how you put them into a suitcase. Now that isn't difficult, is it? Surely even you can do that. Pack it properly!'

Despite my brief moment of silent defiance, I'd been watching Kas carefully because I knew I had to do it *his* way and that I had to get it right. And as I packed the suitcase again with shaking hands, I thought, *Why am I always so stupid? No wonder Kas loses patience with me.*

And then we were in the car, en route for France, and as I sat and watched the sun rising in the sky, I felt a sense of relief that was as overwhelming as it was misplaced.

Chapter 11

I couldn't sleep in the car, and by the time we arrived in southern France, it was midday and I was exhausted. I didn't even think about why Kas wanted to go to France, and I certainly wouldn't have dared to question him if I had. He'd told me I was going to be working there, which I simply accepted was all I needed to know, and the anxiety the prospect raised for me was enough to keep my mind occupied throughout the journey, a significant part of which Kas had spent giving me new instructions.

As we drove along the wide, busy promenade by the sea, he asked me, 'So what do you tell the police if they ask where you're staying?'

'At the Hotel Mirabelle,' I answered, turning to look at him with weary, blood-shot eyes and meeting the full force of his punch on my left cheekbone.

As my head snapped backwards, crashing against the window, Kas roared at me, 'Are you fucking stupid, woman? Why would you tell the police the name of the hotel we're actually staying in? Do you *want* to get us caught?'

What I *wanted* to do was shout at him, 'I'm sick of having to pretend all the time. Before I met you, I never told lies to anyone, and now I rarely tell the truth.' But, instead, I whispered, 'I'm sorry. It's just that … I'm really, really tired.'

When we arrived at the Hotel Mirabelle, my face was red and swollen, but it wasn't the type of hotel where anyone was likely to ask any questions. Most of its clients paid for their rooms by the hour and didn't acknowledge the presence of other guests. After Kas had checked us in, we left our bags and drove around the town so that he could show me the place near some traffic lights on a street parallel to the promenade where I'd be working.

I was petrified that night. I'd been awake for more than 30 hours and I hated Kas for making me go out and work in a strange place while he sat in the hotel or in some bar somewhere, safe and warm and not giving even a moment's thought to what might be happening to me.

I'd almost gone back to square one – not knowing what sort of people to expect as customers and not having any escape routes – and although I'd been happy at the thought of leaving Italy, the reality of being in France was far more frightening than I'd imagined. In Italy, working on the streets had become like playing a game of chess, but in

France it didn't feel like any sort of game at all, and I was very aware that I didn't have any idea what I was doing.

There was a bank next to the traffic lights beside my new spot, a café across the road, which was always closed when I was there, and a block of flats a bit further down. In the darkness, the street would have seemed almost derelict if it hadn't been for the bakery diametrically opposite where I stood, which was open 24 hours a day and which I'd often go to for something to eat before I went back to the hotel in the early hours of the morning.

The first night was very quiet, and the few clients I did have were unremarkable. But I hadn't been out for very long on the second night when I was picked up by a man in a bright red Maserati. He drove to an open-air car park and as soon as he turned off the engine, a car pulled in behind us, illuminating us in the bright beam of its headlights. Immediately, I felt trapped and vulnerable and my heart started to thump. But the guy reached across, put his arm round my shoulders and said, 'It's the police. Pretend you're my girlfriend.' It seemed an odd place for someone who could afford to drive a Maserati to take his girlfriend, but perhaps the policemen didn't care one way or another, because after a few seconds they drove away.

And although that particular guy was all right, he seemed to mark a change in my luck and I had some very weird and unpleasant customers while I was in France. There was one man who picked me up, drove me to a tunnel in an underground car park, gave me 100 Euros and told me to kick him. Even if I hadn't been wearing stiletto-heeled boots, I'd have told him I couldn't do it. But he was insistent, until eventually I agreed. He didn't want me to undress, he didn't want to have sex; he just wanted to sit in the driver's seat, playing with himself and saying 'Harder, harder', while I sat beside him and kicked him, all over his body.

In fact, I don't think I had one single customer who I felt as comfortable with as I did with some of my regulars in Italy, and there seemed to be a disproportionate number of freaks, some of them with sexual habits I'd never even heard of before. So I felt even more uneasy than I might otherwise have done when, after we'd been in France for just three days, Kas announced that he was going to Holland to pick up a delivery of drugs and would be leaving me on my own while he was away.

'I'll only be gone a few days,' he told me. 'You carry on working, and don't forget, if anything happens, if anyone tries to kidnap you, don't fight back. Don't argue with them. Just do as you're told and I'll come and find you.'

I was panic-stricken. It was frightening enough being out on the streets when Kas was just a phone call away, but if there was no one there to help me, I knew I wouldn't stand a chance if anything went wrong. Not fighting back and waiting for Kas to return from Holland didn't constitute a plan that filled me with any confidence. And, judging by all the freaks and weirdos I'd already encountered, something bad happening seemed quite a distinct possibility.

Although I told myself Kas really believed what he was saying – that he'd be able to find me if someone kidnapped me – I think, deep down, I knew he didn't really care about me. He might tell me 'You're the best girl I've ever had', but I knew there were plenty more girls like me and that it wouldn't be difficult for him to find another if he needed to. And it wasn't long before it started to look as though that might be just what he'd have to do, because as soon as he left me alone in France, all hell broke loose.

Although I knew there were other girls working on the streets around where I worked in Italy, I'd rarely encountered any of them. But I saw plenty of others now, and they made it very clear from the outset that they didn't want me there. The first to approach me was a Bulgarian girl who worked from a spot about 50 metres away from the traffic lights. On the night after Kas left, she came stamping across towards me and said, 'You cannot be here. This is not your place to work. Find somewhere else.'

Don't let her see your fear, the voice in my head told me, although it was almost drowned out by another one shouting *Run!* Somehow, though, I managed to stand my ground and look her directly in the eyes as I told her, 'This is my boyfriend's place. I can stay here. My boyfriend is Albanian.'

'Well, my boyfriend is Russian,' she sneered. Then she took another step towards me so that she was standing so close I had to turn my face away from hers, and added, 'He says that this is *my* place.' And, right there on the street, we had a stupid, pointless, scary argument about whose boyfriend was more powerful and more frightening, which ended with the Bulgarian girl saying, 'The Russians control this area. They killed a girl not long ago, so you should watch your back and be very, very careful.'

I didn't know if she was genuinely warning me for my own protection or if she was just trying to frighten me – which she certainly succeeded in doing. The problem was, though, that there wasn't anywhere else I could go, which meant I had a simple choice: stay there, and perhaps be killed by the Russians; or stop working until Kas came back – when he would definitely kill me. So I stood my ground, and eventually the girl walked away and left me alone.

Unfortunately, though, she wasn't the only one who seemed to hate me, and a couple of hours later, the trans-sexual who stood at a spot further down the road came stomping towards me. While her horrible little dog jumped up at me, yapping and scratching my legs with its claws, she shouted in my face, 'We don't want you here. Go away!'

'I am *not* going to leave here,' I told her, hoping my voice conveyed a conviction I didn't feel and trying to shake the wretched little dog off my leg. 'This is where I work. Now leave me alone.'

I didn't dare stop and think about the situation I was in – standing on a street corner in southern France in the middle of the night, arguing with much larger, more streetwise prostitutes about which patch belonged to whom – partly because I didn't want to have to face who

I'd become. Despite my apparent bravado, however, I was really frightened. I knew my presence wasn't welcomed by anyone and that they wouldn't simply leave me alone to get on with it – and alone was exactly what I was.

Fortunately, though, I didn't have any more problems from the other girls that night, which meant that all I had to worry about was what Kas would do to me when he got back from Holland and I had to tell him I hadn't made very much money. So the next night – and all the nights after that – I decided to go out earlier, at 7 instead of 8.30, and to stay out until 5.30 or 6 in the morning.

The night after the Bulgarian girl and transsexual had warned me off, I'd been with a customer and he was driving me back to my spot when I saw the scariest woman I'd ever seen. She was standing on the main promenade, the road that ran parallel to mine, and was probably in her late thirties, about 5 foot 4 inches and at least 14 stone, with a completely shaven head and wearing a short fur coat, low-heeled knee-high boots, a skirt even shorter than her coat and, quite clearly, no bra. She didn't look like someone any man would pay to have sex with and when I described her to one of my clients later that evening, his face became serious as he said, 'I know who you mean. They call her Scary Sue. Stay away from her. She's crazy.'

So my heart sank a little while later when I saw her talking to the Bulgarian girl, and shortly afterwards she came marching round the corner and down the road towards me. She growled something I didn't understand and then started waving her arms and shouting at me. There'd been a cold, persistent drizzle all evening and I was holding my umbrella – the one thing I had that was a link between Jenna and Sophie, because it was the only thing I owned that was pretty and that I might have bought for myself in my previous life. I held it in front of me, like a shield, and began making pathetic little parrying motions with it as I edged away from her.

Over the last couple of nights, I'd seen several girls fighting and standing their ground when other girls attacked them, but I'd never in my entire life been involved in a fight, and it wouldn't even have crossed my mind to try to stand up to Scary Sue. Whenever Kas attacked me, I tried to protect my head with my arms, but I'd never in a million years have thought of trying to hit him or kick out at him. And I knew that my best hope now was to be able to protect my face from this terrifying woman. Instead of assaulting me, though, she reached out one short, stubby-fingered hand, snatched my umbrella, snapped it in two as though it was made of plywood and threw it on the ground at my feet.

Although it hadn't been a great weapon, without it I felt as though I was completely defenceless, and I knew there was a strong possibility that this furious, demented woman was going to kill me. As if to confirm that fear, she suddenly lunged towards me, grabbed a fistful of my hair and started to spin me round and round, kicking at my legs until I fell to my knees on the rain-soaked pavement.

'*Allez, allez, allez!*' she shouted at me, pushing me on to my side and smashing the toe of her boot repeatedly into my ribs before bending down to spit several times in my face. It felt as though my body was going to explode, but then, through the pain of hazy, fading consciousness, I heard the screech of tyres and a man's voice shouting in English, 'Get in! Get *in!*' My head was pounding and as I tried to stand up, I felt sick. But, somehow, I managed to scrabble to my feet and stumble towards the open door of the car, and then I felt hands reaching out and dragging me onto the passenger seat.

As the car sped away down the road, I glanced in the wing mirror and could see Scary Sue running after it, waving her arms again and shouting words that, mercifully, I couldn't hear.

'Are you all right? Are you hurt?' the driver of the car asked me. But I couldn't clear my head enough to answer him.

I was always covered in bruises because of what Kas did to me, but this time the pain was different. It felt as though burning hot liquid was flowing into every part of my body. Every single one of my muscles was throbbing and every inch of my skin was sore and tender, so that I could barely move. I lay my head back against the seat and moaned, and when the man reached across in front of me, I didn't even have the energy to react. I didn't know who he was or why he'd picked me up when he did, but I was completely defenceless; whatever happened to me now was beyond my control. He must have seen me flinch because as he opened the glove compartment and took out a pack of tissues and a small bottle, he said, 'It's okay. I'm not going to hurt you. Take this. Clean yourself up. It'll sting on those cuts, I'm afraid. But I guess that's nothing compared to what you've just been through.' And that's when I started to cry.

'I'm scared,' I whimpered. 'She's going to kill me.'

'That does seem to be a possibility,' the man said, wryly. 'Clearly, you can't go back there tonight. Come on, cheer up. You're safe for now at least.'

After a few minutes, he stopped the car and pulled in to the side of the road, turning off the engine while he helped me to clean myself up. Then he lit a cigarette, placed it carefully in my shaking hand and said, 'You have to be careful. You've got to stay away from her. She's mad and she's not going to leave you alone now. Obviously she doesn't like you, but most of all she doesn't like the fact that you're here. None of the girls wants you here. You don't look right. You don't fit in.'

He spoke such good English that I hadn't previously noticed the slight French accent I could hear now, and I wondered how he'd known *I* was English and whether his arrival on the scene just in time to prevent Scary Sue from killing me was chance, or if he was someone Kas had asked to watch out for me while he was away. Either way, it didn't really matter. I was just extremely glad he'd arrived when he did.

'Come on,' he said, hooking a strand of hair behind my ear and patting my knee. 'You need to eat. We'll get some food.'

And, surprisingly, he was right – food was exactly what I needed, and I sat opposite him at a table in a pizza restaurant near the harbour eating as though I'd never seen food before, while he sipped a glass of wine and watched me. Then he paid for my meal and dropped me off on a road not far away from my usual spot.

I'd earned almost nothing that night and I knew I had to go back to work, but it didn't take me long to realise it was hopeless. I was in so much agony I couldn't even turn my head. So I crept back to the hotel and lay in a warm bath, thinking, *This is the worst day of all the worst days of my life. If she sees me again, I'm dead. I've got to stay out of her way.*

I was expecting her to come after me again the next night, and I was surprised when I didn't see her, or the following night either. There was a group of transsexuals who worked on a road at right-angles to mine and who, when I asked them, said they were happy for me to work nearby. But, a couple of hours later, two Albanian girls came running at me, shouting, 'No, *no*, go away, go away,' and I had to move on.

I was constantly on the alert, watching and listening. I'd get customers to drop me off on another road and then I'd walk back to my spot along an indirect route, scanning every side street I passed and jumping at every shadow.

On the third night after Scary Sue had attacked me, I was picked up at about 2 o'clock in the morning by a man who drove a short distance along the promenade and parked in a small cove next to the sea. He seemed awkward and ill at ease, but as most of my customers were strange in one way or another, I didn't really take much notice. What *was* odd, though, was that he didn't want to have sex, and he even appeared to be reluctant for me to do it by hand. I just wanted to get it over with as quickly as possible, so although I heard the sound of footsteps approaching the car, it didn't really register because I'd already switched off my thoughts and let my mind go blank.

I always told customers to lock the car doors when we stopped – although I couldn't remember afterwards whether I'd actually said it that time. But suddenly the door beside me flew open and what felt like a dozen hands reached in, pinching and pulling at my body and dragging me out of the car by my hair.

As I hit the ground, I looked up and saw the two Albanian girls who'd been spoiling for a fight the previous night. They began to kick me viciously and as I tried to curl into a ball to protect my face and stomach, I shouted in French to the guy in the car, 'Help me! *Please.* They're going to kill me.' But he didn't move, and when I glanced up at him, he looked steadily back at me, shrugged and said, '*Non, je suis desolé.* [No, I'm sorry.]' And I knew that the moment I'd been dreading had come.

Luckily, though – I don't know if it was because she felt sorry for me or because she realised they might actually kill me – one of them suddenly stopped kicking me and pulled her friend off. 'Go. Just go,' she told me, and I managed to stand up and stumble back towards the main road, too shocked even to cry.

I found out later what I'd already strongly suspected – that the attack had been masterminded by Scary Sue. She'd wanted to send me a message, and I got it, loud and clear, although I still didn't understand why my presence bothered her so much; I'd never had any trouble like that in Italy. But I wasn't in any position to argue. In future, I'd have to be extra vigilant, although, ultimately, there was little I could do if she was determined to make it impossible for me to work in the area.

The French guy who spoke almost perfect English and had saved me from Scary Sue's first attack came back several times while Kas was away. He just seemed to appear out of nowhere when I was in trouble, and I began to wonder who he was. I hoped he was someone Kas had asked to keep an eye on me, although he might just have been lonely and/or enjoyed playing the hero, or maybe he was an undercover cop. Whoever he was, I knew I couldn't trust him, both because he might have been trying to take me over to work for him, and because Kas had taught me well and I wouldn't have risked trusting anyone.

He arrived just as I got back to my spot after the Albanian girls had attacked me. I don't really know what made me think I'd be able to work again that night. My whole body was sore and there was an agonising pain in my stomach, which made me wince as I lifted my foot off the ground to get into his car.

'Are you okay?' he asked. 'You look terrible.' And when I told him what had happened, he sighed and said, 'Listen, she doesn't want you here. Word has spread and everyone knows about you now, so they'll all be on the look-out for you. You'll have to find somewhere else. I told you, you don't look right. You don't fit.'

'But I don't know what you mean,' I wailed. 'I may not look like Scary Sue or the transsexuals, but I'm no different from most of the other girls.' And it was a thought that made me suddenly sad.

'But you *are*,' he said. 'For one thing, you don't dress right and your hair isn't right. But look, don't worry. I can help you. Just give me your phone number.'

'*No!*' I was instantly wary, although fortunately he didn't seem to be offended by the way I'd spoken.

'Okay, well let's meet somewhere tomorrow and I'll take you to buy some new clothes and get a haircut,' he said.

Maybe my clothes *were* out of place there and maybe what he was suggesting would have made a difference, but I refused his offer. I doubted any of the people I encountered had purely good intentions towards me and I knew that, even if he did and I accepted his help, Kas would kill me when he came back. So I was relieved when, instead of pushing me, the man shrugged and said, 'I've asked around to see if there's any way of helping you. There's an area a bit further down the road that's run by Lithuanians. It's actually a woman who's in charge and I asked her if you could go and work there, but she won't have you either.'

Why? I thought. *Why are you getting involved in my business? What difference does it make to you? Who are you?*

Having someone there who was offering me help I couldn't accept was almost worse than having no one at all. I hugged my arms against my chest, bending forward slightly to try to ease the pain in my stomach, and felt completely alone and exhausted. I'd been beaten up and harassed because I was being forced to fight for my 'right' to do something I didn't even want to do, and I'd almost forgotten what it was like to be Sophie. When I'd told the man that I was just like all the other girls, I'd believed it – and it was true, because I'd had to *become* Jenna in order to stand any chance at all of being able to survive.

There was another man who came a few times and was kind to me too. He was about my age and good-looking and he asked me questions about myself. But although I think he was genuine, every time I told him something I'd start to panic, because I was frightened in case I'd said too much. One night, he came late, when I'd already made quite a lot of money, so we just sat in his car, chatting, and it was really nice to have someone to talk to about normal, everyday things. Then he asked me if I was working on my own.

'People think you are,' he said. 'You must be careful. You must make sure they know you've got someone to protect you. This is a violent place – you won't survive on your own.'

I was surprised at how disappointed I felt at the thought that he, too, might have an ulterior motive for being nice to me and that perhaps he just wanted to find out who was controlling me. But at least he *was* nice, whereas most of the men who picked me up were horrible.

One night, a car drove past me with three or four people in it, and then a little while later the driver came back on his own. His driving was erratic and there was something odd about him, although I couldn't work out what it was. He was friendly enough, but tense, and I wondered if he was high on drugs. I felt uncomfortable sitting beside him because it seemed as though there was *something* bubbling away beneath the surface – anger, maybe – and that it might burst out at any moment.

He chatted to me in French and asked me questions as he drove, and I tried to sound friendly when I answered them. And then I just happened to glance down and see the screwdriver he was holding in his hand. I knew I mustn't say anything or show my fear, although I was unable to block out the thought that he was going to kill me.

Panic was flooding through me, but although I tried to stay calm and answer his questions in a normal voice, he must have sensed something, because he suddenly turned his head to look at me and asked, '*What?* What's wrong?' I pointed to the screwdriver and he laughed as he said, 'Ah, no. It's okay,' and put it down on the ledge underneath the dashboard.

Perhaps he *had* been thinking about attacking me, or perhaps he'd been afraid that *I* might try to rob *him*. Or maybe holding the screwdriver in his hand had had no purpose at all and had simply been the random act of someone whose mind was disturbed. Whatever the reason, although I was lucky on that occasion, it was just another reminder – had I needed one – that I was always only one step away from real danger and completely at the mercy of the strangers and oddballs who picked me up.

Another customer refused to go to the place I told him to go to. Trying not to sound afraid, I demanded he stop the car and let me out. But he just ignored me and kept driving, and after 15 minutes we were some distance out of town. I didn't know where I was or how to get back to the main road, and I was struggling to at least appear calm. I'd told him '50 Euros' before I'd got into the car and when he finally stopped, in a garage full of shuttered parking spaces, and I told him he must give it to me first, he kept insisting '*Après* [Afterwards],' and tried to rip the clothes off my body. I began to scream and kick out at him, banging with my fists on everything in sight, until eventually he gave up and, to my surprise, took me back to where he'd picked me up.

When I think about it now, I realise how odd it must seem to other people that I didn't try to escape while Kas was away, and the reasons are difficult to explain. I think that the way people like Kas control people like me involves a sort of brainwashing. When he said that he'd take my brothers if I didn't do what he told me to do, and that wherever I tried to hide, he'd find me, I believed him. Just as I believed him when he said I shouldn't trust anyone because he had friends everywhere, including among the police, and that even if I did escape, I wouldn't be able to take care of myself because I was too stupid.

Kas was away for about a week, and by the time he came back I was completely shattered. Having to rely on my own instincts and reactions because there was no one there to back me up when things went wrong had been exhausting. So I suppose, in some small way, I was glad when he came back, although I was dreading having to tell him what had been happening and explain why I hadn't made as much money as he'd expected me to.

'I tried to work after I'd been beaten up,' I told him. 'But my whole body was so bruised I could barely move, so I had to come back to the hotel.'

As he hit me across the head, he shouted at me, 'Why are you lying to me, woman? Are you so stupid that you think I believe these lies?'

I fell backwards against the bed, trying not to cry, because I knew the sight of my tears would only enrage him further. As I pushed up the sleeve of my top and held out my arm for him to see, I said, 'I'm *not* lying, I promise. Look at me. My entire body is covered in bruises. Why would I lie to you?'

He bent down, twisted his fingers in my hair and pulled me to my feet, hissing into my face, 'Don't *ever* forget that I have people watching you. You will never know who they are or where they are.' Then he began to fire questions at me: Where were you at this time? What were you doing between this hour and that one? And I felt faint with fear. What should I tell him I was doing when I was eating pizza in a restaurant with the man who'd rescued me from Scary Sue?

I rarely dared to lie to Kas, but I knew I couldn't tell him the truth. So I told him I'd managed to escape and had gone back to the hotel to clean myself up, but that I'd been too bruised and sore to go out again. My whole body was shaking as I told the lie, and for a moment I wondered if he *could* actually read my thoughts, or if perhaps he already knew the truth because someone he knew had seen me in the restaurant that night. By some miracle, however, I got away with it, although he still shouted at me for 'getting into a fight' with Scary Sue in the first place and for risking drawing attention to him. He told me I was stupid, that he couldn't ever trust me and that one day, he knew, I would get him into trouble.

'Now *I* have to fight with people because of you,' he shouted angrily. 'I have to sort out the mess you've created because of your incompetence and because you can't look after yourself for even a couple of days. This is *your* fault.'

Later that evening, he shrugged as he told me, 'Just keep doing what you've been doing – getting picked up in one place and dropped off in another. And try not to let her see you.' It wasn't the solution to the problem I'd been hoping for, but at least I wouldn't be entirely on my own anymore.

I remained constantly alert and on the look-out for Scary Sue and then, one night, a car drove very slowly past me and I could see her in the passenger seat, making throat-cutting motions with her hand. For one dread-filled moment I thought the car was going to stop, and perhaps it might have done if another car hadn't pulled up beside me at that moment. I jumped into it, almost shouting at the bewildered driver 'Go, go, *go!*', and he sped away. I saw her again several times that night, and I knew that, eventually, I'd make a mistake and then I'd turn around and she'd be there.

Two nights later, a man came to me on foot, wanting me to go with him to a hotel. Although the request in itself wasn't unusual, no one had ever picked me up without a car before, and I was immediately wary. I felt uncomfortable just standing talking to him, but there seemed to be no concrete reason to turn him down – and I knew Kas expected me to make up at least some of the money I'd lost while he was away. So I told the man it would cost 200 Euros, and he didn't even pause to consider the amount before saying, 'Okay, we'll go to the cash machine.'

I walked along the road behind him feeling increasingly uneasy, and then he turned his head to say something to me over his shoulder and I realised he was Russian.

'No Russians. Never go with Russians. They're trouble,' Kas was forever telling me. My heart started to race and I dropped back a few steps. And as soon as he stepped up to the cash machine, I turned and began to run. I could hear him shouting after me, 'Come back! Wait!' But I just kept running and running until I reached the hotel.

My head was pounding and I didn't seem able to catch my breath as I tried to tell Kas what had happened. But he held up his hand to cut short my explanation and barked at me, 'You've already caused me enough trouble here. We're going back to Italy tomorrow.'

Looking back on it now, I don't think it was a decision Kas had made because of the trouble he said I'd caused; I think it was what he'd always intended to do. But, whatever the reason, it probably saved my life. I'd been in France for 14 days – although it had seemed at least twice as long – and I was even more relieved to be going back to Italy than I'd been when we left there, because I don't think I'd have managed to survive for much longer. I was dodging too many bullets and I knew that, eventually, one of them was going to hit me.

Chapter 12

As soon as we arrived back in Italy, I went straight out to work. This time, though, it was different, because I was going back to a place I knew, where there were people I recognised, and some I even liked, and where there'd be no men with screwdrivers or crazy women trying to kill me. I hadn't forgotten the dangers that did exist, but somehow, after all the madness of France, they didn't seem to be quite so scary anymore.

In France, I hadn't fitted in, but back in Italy I felt as though I knew the score: I knew how to dodge the police and that – mostly – nothing terrible would happen when I didn't succeed. I knew what type of men to avoid and I had my regular clients, who were genuinely glad to see me when I got back. It felt almost like coming home – at least, as long as I didn't think about my *real* home and my family. But my relief proved to be short-lived and it wasn't long before things started to go wrong again.

Kas was doing a lot of drug deals and he knew that the police were looking for him. So, one day, he moved me out of the flat and into a room in a sleazy hotel, where I stayed for the next couple of weeks, sometimes on my own and sometimes with Kas there too.

I hadn't been feeling well for some time. I was often queasy and dizzy, and every time I looked in the mirror I had a strangely disorientated sensation. I hated seeing my reflection staring blankly back at me, I hated the clothes I wore, and I hated the fact that I was ugly-thin, and so run down I kept getting sick. It didn't matter to Kas how ill I was, though; he just told me to pull myself together and go to work.

Before long, I seemed to have developed an almost never-ending cold and there was one night, when my eyes were red and puffy and I could hardly breathe, when my nose began to run while I was having sex with a man and he stopped and handed me a tissue. I felt sick with self-disgust. I'd learned almost to close my mind to what I was doing, but somehow, in that moment, I felt as though I'd just lost the very last remnants of my self-respect.

The nights were bitterly cold by that time and I never seemed to be able to get warm. My feet and hands were always numb and I shivered constantly. I was exhausted too. But it wasn't the sort of tiredness that a good long sleep might have cured; I was absolutely and utterly worn out. I walked around like a zombie, following Kas's instructions and barely able to think for myself.

Sometimes I couldn't believe it was possible that I could go on living like that, and those were the times when I became really frightened, because I couldn't see any future at all, and I thought that must mean I was going to die. One night, a client who was a doctor told me, 'You can't stay out here like this. You've got pneumonia. You *have* to stop. You must go to the hospital and get some treatment.'

'I can't,' I told him. 'It doesn't matter. I'll be all right.'

'No, you *won't*,' he said, and he touched my shoulder in a kind, fatherly sort of way that made me want to burst into tears. 'You won't be all right if you don't get medical attention *now*.'

When I went back to the hotel that night, I told Kas what the man had said and asked him if I could stop working, just for a few days until I was better. But he shouted at me, 'For a cold? What's wrong with you, woman? What's your problem? Why are you making such a drama out of a little cold?'

'It *isn't* just a cold though,' I told him, in a voice that sounded pathetically child-like. 'I feel so ill and weak and it's frightening when I can't breathe properly.'

'It's your own fault,' he told me, slapping me across the head. 'You wouldn't keep getting sick if you ate properly.'

Maybe he was right, but I simply couldn't eat, no matter how much I wanted to, because anything other than a few mouthfuls of bland food made me sick. For months my life had been a constantly repeated cycle of work, sleep, eat, work, sleep, eat ... I never saw daylight, and when I woke up I was just as tired as I had been when I'd gone to bed.

I did gradually get better, though – and then immediately I fell ill again. I started getting terrible stomach pains, which grew steadily worse and worse until I began to wonder whether my bowel might have become twisted again, as it had been when I'd had to have an operation instead of going to Albania to marry Erion – what seemed like a whole lifetime ago.

One night, the pain was so bad that when I had sex it felt as though a red-hot poker was being pushed up inside me. I began to sweat and had to grip the sides of the seat so tightly to stop myself pushing the man away that I thought my fingers were going to snap.

I don't know how I got through the rest of that night, and when I went back to the hotel I told Kas, 'I can't do it anymore. You have no idea how much it hurts. I can't bear the pain.'

The next night, the pain was even worse and I tried to detach my mind from my body by repeating over and over again in my head, like a mantra, the words, *It won't kill you. It's only pain.* I think I must have begun to look ill, though, because Kas drove me to work the following night – which was something he rarely bothered to do by that time – and as he was dropping me off he said, 'I've been speaking to a friend and his girlfriend sometimes gets the same thing. It's just a urine infection. You need to drink more water and try to do more oral.' But that night was the worst of all, and I was with what was probably my fifteenth customer when the pain became so intense that I didn't care what Kas did to me, I knew I couldn't carry on and I blurted out, 'Stop! *Please!* I can't do this. I'm sorry.'

It took far longer than usual for me to walk back to the hotel, and all the time I was trying not to think about how Kas would react. I knew he'd be angry because I'd stopped work early, but there was nothing I could do to change that, so I was amazed when he took one look at me and told me to go to bed.

I desperately wanted to sleep, but the pain kept waking me up, and when I heard Kas go out the next morning, I dragged myself out of bed, got dressed and walked out of the hotel and down the road. I didn't know where he'd gone or how long he'd be out, and I could only walk slowly, looking around anxiously all the time, expecting at any moment to see his car driving along the road towards me.

When I finally stepped through the double glass doors of the main entrance of the local hospital, I was on the verge of passing out. I remember someone rushing forward and putting her arm around my waist and the next thing I was aware of was opening my eyes and looking up into a bright, almost white, light that was shining from some-where above my head. In fact, I was lying on a trolley in a curtained cubicle and after I'd been examined by a doctor, I was taken by ambulance to another hospital on the other side of town, where I was examined again, admitted to a ward and put on a drip.

Then a woman in a white coat came and stood beside my bed, looked at me with a grave, but not unkind, expression and told me she was a gynaecologist. She spoke good English and asked me lots of questions, including, 'How often do you have sex?'

'Not often,' I answered, looking away from her as I told the lie. 'But when I do, it's really painful.'

She touched the back of my hand gently and smiled a small, rueful smile as she said, 'We're going to keep you here for a while. You need to get some rest and, more importantly, you need fluids. You're dehydrated. But you *have* to stay here. Do you understand?'

I nodded my head and, despite my blush of embarrassment, felt a great wave of weariness and relief wash over me as I thought, *She knows. Thank God, because I can't do this anymore.*

The Italian mobile phone Kas had given me had been in the pocket of my jacket, but someone must have taken it out when I'd put on the hospital gown I'd been given, because after the doctor had gone, I noticed it lying on top of the little cupboard beside my bed. I reached out my hand and picked it up, and then sat for a while, just looking at it, before ringing Kas's number and whispering, 'I'm in the hospital.'

The possibility of not phoning him didn't even cross my mind at the time. I was completely conditioned to do what he told me to do, even when he wasn't there, and even when going against that conditioning might have meant he'd never have found me and I would have had the chance to escape from him. It's hard to explain, but defying him simply wasn't an option.

I was terrified of him and I was like an obedient child – or a puppet on a string, and he was the puppet master. I'd quickly learned to accept as normal the fact that Kas decided everything on my behalf, and for the last few months I had made almost no decisions of my own. If he told me to eat, I ate; and I asked his permission before doing anything: Can I go to the toilet? Can I wear this? Can I smoke a cigarette? Can I listen to music? And if he said no, I didn't even consider going against him, any more than I considered not phoning him from the hospital to let him know where I was.

Kas went crazy, as I'd known he would. 'How *dare* you?' he shouted. 'How dare you go there without asking me?' And then, abruptly, he seemed to calm down and he sounded almost concerned as he asked, 'What have they said to you? You're going to be okay, aren't you, little mouse? I'll take better care of you in the future, I promise. I'll come to the hospital.' Then his tone changed again and he said angrily, 'But you should have told me. You shouldn't have just gone on your own. You *have* to do what I tell you to do. Do you understand? It's very important. You won't forget it again, will you?'

'No, I'm sorry,' I said. 'It was just … I felt so ill.' But in my head a voice was screaming, *Don't come. Please don't come to the hospital. Please, God, let something happen so that he doesn't come.* And although my prayer wasn't answered, at least he didn't visit me until the next day – and then he only stayed for 10 minutes.

There was only one other woman on the ward, a couple of beds away, and Kas spoke quietly so that she couldn't hear what he was saying as he hissed into my ear, 'There are *Carabinieri* all over the hospital. Do you have any idea how much trouble I could get into if anyone saw me here?' Then, speaking at a normal level, he said, 'I need to go now. I'll come back tomorrow. In the meantime, you must stay here and sleep, and make sure you eat.'

In fact, I slept for most of the next 24 hours and not long after I woke up the doctor came to see me. 'We're in a very difficult situation,' she told me. 'As you're British, you shouldn't have to pay for your treatment or for being here in hospital, but because you don't have any ID, the cost could be 10,000 Euros, or even more.'

I was horrified. Kas had my passport and I felt trapped. What on earth was I going to do? Tears began to well up in my eyes, and the doctor patted my hand as she added hastily, 'But don't worry about that now. We need to concentrate on getting you well again. There'll be plenty of time to work something out later.'

Kas arrived about an hour after the doctor had been, and when I told him what she'd said, he sat down on the bed beside me and whispered, 'I'm going to get you out of here tomorrow.'

'But I *can't* leave,' I said, instantly regretting having spoken so quickly and having allowed the fear to be so clearly audible in my voice. The blood was pounding in my ears and I had to struggle to focus on Kas's face when I looked at him. 'I mean because I've got a drip in my arm,' I added hastily.

He glanced towards the woman in the other bed, smiled pleasantly at her and then, putting his arm around my shoulders and his mouth close to my ear, hissed at me, 'You think a fucking drip is a problem? I'll rip it out of your arm myself if I have to.'

Although he appeared to be stroking my hair, what he was actually doing was pulling it so hard that my neck was twisted. He dug his fingernails into my scalp and, with his other hand, jabbed the tips of his car keys into my thigh as he whispered, 'Whatever you do, do not tell anyone where you are. Do you understand? Do not even *think* about telling your mother.'

'I won't. I promise,' I said. I was trying to sound calm, but my heart was thudding and I felt sick, because the truth was that I'd already phoned my mother. I'd called her after the doctor had been in to see me earlier that afternoon, because I was frightened and because it had suddenly seemed really important that someone who actually cared about me knew where I was and that I wasn't well.

'How's Auntie Linda?' I'd whispered to my mother as

soon as she answered the phone, and her voice had been hoarse with emotion as she answered, 'We're going to visit her tonight.' And that's when I'd started to cry, because I knew that my mother and stepfather would be leaving home that night to come and find me.

'I'm in a hospital,' I told my mother. 'But don't worry; I'll be fine. It's just that …' I paused for a moment and blew my nose to try to stop the flow of tears. 'It's just that I haven't got my passport with me and I need insurance. I don't know what to do.'

She told me not to worry, that she'd work something out, and then she asked me, 'Is he violent towards you, Sophie?' and I began to sob as I whispered, 'Yes.'

Now, though, with Kas sitting on my bed, all I could think was, *Oh my God, I'm in so much trouble. He'll kill me if he finds out what I've done.*

'You fucking dare try anything and you'll see what I'll do to you,' Kas was saying. 'You think these people are here to help you? They don't care about you; no one cares about you except me, so don't fuck with me. I will come tomorrow and take you out of here and if you say a word to anyone, I'll kill you and then your precious mother will never see you again.'

The woman in the other bed glanced towards us and Kas patted my arm and kissed my cheek as he mouthed at me again, 'Don't fuck with me.' Then he left, and as I lay back on the bed and cried, the thought went round and round in my head: *If he finds out, I'm dead.*

Suddenly, it was as though all the tension had drained out of me and I felt almost calm. I was, quite literally, *tired* of being afraid and, in any case, the reality was that whatever happened now was out of my control. I couldn't fight back against Kas – I was too weak and too exhausted. But, before I gave up, I desperately wanted to hear my mother's voice again. So I dialled her number, although all I managed to say before I burst into tears was 'Oh, Mum!'

I could tell that my mother was crying too as she told me, 'It's all right, Sophie. We're coming. We're on our way. We've already booked a ferry. We tried to get a flight, but we were too late to get anything today or tomorrow morning, so we're driving. We're leaving now. But listen to me, darling. This is very, *very* important. Do *not* tell him we're coming.'

'But Mum, he's taking me out of the hospital tomorrow,' I sobbed.

'*No!* You mustn't leave,' my mother shrieked. 'We'll be there tomorrow. Sophie, you *have* to wait for us.'

'But what if he gets here first?' I could feel the panic building up inside me so that I couldn't breathe. 'Oh Mum, don't let him take me. Please Mum, *please*. Get here before he does.'

For the rest of that day and the night that followed, my mind was numb. All I could think about was my fear and every time I fell asleep, I had the same dream, in which my mother and stepfather were running down the corridors of the hospital calling my name while I sat beside Kas in his car as he drove out of the car park and into the traffic.

During the afternoon of the next day, Kas sent me a text message saying he'd had to take his car to the garage but that he'd be at the hospital within the next couple of hours. I was already on the verge of hysteria and I was shaking and stammering when I phoned my mother to tell her.

'Just try to hold on, Sophie,' she said. 'We've spoken to someone at the embassy and they've contacted the hospital, so they know we're coming. They already suspected something was wrong and they've said they'll try to keep you there until we arrive.'

'Hurry, Mum,' I sobbed. 'Please hurry. I'm *so* frightened.'

Two hours later, I had a phone call from Kas to tell me he was almost at the hospital and then another shortly afterwards from Mum saying, 'We're five minutes away.'

'When you see him, don't say anything,' I pleaded with my mother. 'You don't know him, Mum. You have no idea who he is. If you upset him or cause any trouble, you can't imagine what the consequences might be. So, please, just act as though everything's normal.'

It felt as though I was holding a bomb in my hands, waiting for it to explode. Kas had told me many times what he'd do to my little brothers if I disobeyed him in any way, and I'd seen some of what he was capable of when he attacked the man who'd overstepped the line with me, so I was in no doubt that he meant what he said.

He hadn't ever met my mum, but in the early days, before I stopped talking about anything, I'd talked about her a lot and he used to say to me, nastily, 'Oh your *mum!* You always do what your *mum* tells you to do. She's controlling your mind.' Which was nonsense, and ironic considering that that was precisely what he was doing.

'It'll be all right, I promise,' Mum said. 'But you *must not* leave the hospital. Do you understand, Sophie? Do *not* leave.' And then she gave one, heart-rending sob as she added, 'You've *got* to stay where you are, Sophie, or I might never see you again.'

For the next few minutes, I sat in the chair beside my bed, watching the door and praying, *Please let it be Mum. Please, please, please God, don't let Kas walk through the door first.* And then there he was, pushing open the door and walking towards my bed.

I could see from his expression that he knew immediately something was wrong and as I stood up, trying to suppress my instinct to back away from him, I blurted out, 'My mum's here.'

Two nurses had come to the ward a little while earlier and taken the other woman away, so Kas no longer had to fake a smile or whisper when he said, 'You fucking *what?*'

'My mum,' I told him again, swallowing hard and clenching my fists to try to stop my body shaking. 'I didn't have any insurance and I couldn't pay for the hospital, so I thought that if I rang my mum, she could ask my sister to phone an insurance company in England and pretend to be me and then she could get some insurance in my name. Then Mum and Steve were worried about me ...' I was speaking quickly, the words tumbling out of my mouth in an almost incoherent torrent, partly because I was incapable of stopping them and partly because I was trying to buy myself some time. 'They came because they need to get me home and I can't fly,' I continued, not giving Kas a chance to interject. 'The doctors won't let me fly because of my stomach and that's why Mum and my stepdad have come to drive me home.'

To my amazement, Kas seemed to accept what I was telling him – or perhaps he realised that if my mother and Steve *were* about to arrive at the hospital, he'd have to play a clever game to make sure that they left again without me. And just as he was shrugging and saying 'Okay', the door of the ward burst open and my mother almost flew through it, followed by Steve, who was striding more slowly but very purposefully in her wake, his jaw set and his face impassive, except for a frown that gave him an air of absolute determination.

Kas turned towards them as they came through the door and although he smiled his most charming smile and greeted them politely, neither of them spoke to him. In fact, I could tell immediately that my mother couldn't even bring herself to look at him, and when she almost ran across the room and wrapped her arms around me, I broke down and began to sob.

I was shaking uncontrollably, but suddenly I felt over-whelmed by exhaustion and by an almost palpable sense of relief at the realisation that I was no longer totally alone. Often during the last few months, when I'd listened, my head bowed in dejected acceptance, as Kas shouted at me for one failing or another, or I'd stood, shivering with cold and abject misery at the side of the road, waiting for the next stranger to stop his car beside me, I'd dreamed about looking up and seeing my mum. And now, as the warmth of her body seemed to radiate into mine, I was a little girl again, waking up from a nightmare and knowing that as long as my mother's arms were around me, nothing could hurt me.

Then I remembered that even though Mum and Steve were there, I was still a long way from being safe. I knew Kas would go to almost any lengths to keep me under his control, and I was frightened at the thought of what he might do if he became suspicious about their real inten-tions. Although Steve appeared to be calm and unemo-tional, I knew he would be assessing and processing everything and everyone around him so that he could make an informed decision about what to do. And I could feel the tension in my mother's body as she fought to control the desire to tear Kas apart with her bare hands, even though she didn't have any idea of what he'd really done to me. So I was afraid they might say or do some-thing that would make Kas angry – because if that happened, I knew I would never escape.

But, although I wasn't aware of it at the time, Mum and Steve already understood that Kas was more than just a man who bullied and threatened his girlfriends. After talking to someone at the British Embassy, they'd decided that, whatever happened, they were going to keep their cool and outwit him, because the only thing that mattered to them was getting me away from him.

I was still wrapped in my mother's arms when the door from the corridor was pushed open again and a nurse came bustling in. Smiling at us briskly, she said, in broken English, 'We clean this room now. You must be outside.' Then she pointed towards my mother and me and added, 'Not you.' Kas spoke rapidly to her in Italian, but she shrugged and ushered him and Steve out into the corridor just as a small, grey-haired woman in an overall came in and began to mop the floor.

As soon as the door closed behind Kas and Steve, my mother said to me, 'Just follow my lead and do whatever Steve and I say.' I could see the shocked distress in her eyes as she looked at me, and for the first time I tried to imagine what my emaciated body, dark-rimmed eyes and gaunt face must look like to someone who hadn't seen me for six months.

There was little time for her to say much more before the door opened again and the nurse told us, 'The doctor wants to talk with you.'

When we went out into the corridor, Kas and Steve were standing silently a few feet apart from each other, both with similarly stern, uncompromising expressions on their faces. But as soon as he saw us, Kas became instantly charming and full of concern. 'I will come with you to see the doctor,' he told my mother. 'I speak Italian – I can translate for you.' He moved towards her, but instantly Steve stepped between them and, speaking slowly in an impassive monotone, said, 'Now listen, lad. This is a family matter and you are not a member of this family, so I will ask you kindly, if you don't mind, to wait over there.' He pointed towards a row of chairs that were neatly aligned along one wall of the corridor. 'Please allow us to sort this out. She's our daughter and we don't need anyone to translate for us, thank you very much.'

I saw the flash of anger in Kas's eyes and I was suddenly very afraid for all of us. Steve had no idea who he was dealing with, but I'd forgotten that his own quiet stoicism hid a determination every bit as steely as Kas's own. And as Kas stepped aside to let us pass, Steve turned his back on him and walked between my mother and me down the corridor and into the office where the doctor was waiting for us.

'We need copies of your drivers' licences,' the doctor told my parents. 'Then just take her home. When you've got her there safely, send us a copy of her passport, but don't worry about that now.'

My mother had no idea what had happened to me during the last six months, but she said later that when she shook the doctor's hand and looked into his eyes, she realised that, whatever it was, *he* knew.

'But Kas has got my passport,' I said. 'I can't ...'

'Yes you can, love.' Steve put his hand on my shoulder. 'You've come this far. You can do this one last thing. And this time, we'll be there right beside you.'

Other than my passport, I had very few possessions at the hotel, and even fewer that I wanted to take home with me, and I dreaded the thought of having to go back there. I still didn't really believe I was going to escape from Kas, and I was afraid that the longer we were with him, the more time he'd have to think of some plan to snatch me away from Mum and Steve again, and then any chance I might have had of escaping would be lost.

'You come with me,' Kas told me, putting his hand on my arm and smiling a charming smile that didn't reach his eyes.

'*No!*' My mother almost shouted the word at him. Then she paused, took a deep breath and said, in a more even tone, 'She should come with us. It's been such a long time since we last saw her.'

'Ah, but if you're going to take her away from me for a while, it would be nice for me if she could come in my car, so that I can be with her one last time before she goes,' Kas said.

Again my mother said 'No'. But, looking directly into her eyes, I told her, 'It's okay, I'll go with Kas.'

Mum had told Kas that the doctor recommended taking me back to England to give me a chance to recover fully from my illness, but I couldn't understand why he seemed to be accepting what was happening. Perhaps it was simply because he knew he could get me back whenever he wanted to. Although what I wanted more than anything in the world was to escape from him, I was fixated on the idea that we mustn't give him any reason to suspect I wasn't planning on coming back. I was terrified, too, that the longer we were there, the more chance there was of one of us saying or doing something to arouse his suspicions and make him change his mind. So it just seemed best to do what he wanted and not waste precious time arguing with him, particularly as I knew that once he'd decided on something, his determination was unshakeable.

In the car, Kas told me that he would book a flight for my return to Italy. 'Four weeks should be plenty of time for you to get better,' he said. 'And if you give me your credit card and PIN number, I'll have a little deposit in case you get any ideas about not coming back.' Then his voice became cold and threatening as he added, 'And don't even think about giving me the wrong PIN number. Just wait and see what I'll do to you if you try to trick me. Don't ever think that I'm not with you or that I won't be able to find you, wherever you go.' And I had no doubt that what he said was true.

Steve and Mum followed us to the hotel and as Kas turned into the driveway, Steve quickly reversed his car in too, directly behind Kas's so that he was blocking the exit. Then, almost before he'd turned off the engine, he jumped out and opened the boot, standing slightly to one side so that Kas couldn't avoid seeing what he was doing as he moved the heavy metal snow chains to one side. He looked at Kas steadily for a moment before turning to me and saying cheerfully, 'Right, love. You've got 10 minutes and then we're leaving. Your mum and I will wait here.'

In the horrible little hotel room, Kas stood watching me while I put some clothes into a suitcase and tried not to show how frightened I was. I was acutely aware that I was throwing things into the case in the way that had previously made him so angry, and as I quickly folded a jumper, a piece of paper fell out of the pocket. Kas bent down, picked it up, glanced at it and suddenly reached out and hit me, hard, across the head with his open hand.

'What the *fuck* is this?' he shouted, slapping me again and then punching me with his tightly clenched fist.

'I … I don't know,' I stammered, trying to focus on the bit of paper he was holding just a couple of inches in front of my eyes. At first, I couldn't make any sense of the numbers that were written on it – clearly in my handwriting. And then I remembered the night when freezing cold rain had been falling steadily for hours and I'd tried to figure out whether I'd earned enough money to be able to stop work early and find somewhere dry to hide until it was time to go back to the hotel.

'Are you trying to get me caught, woman?' Kas hit me again. 'You better straighten up before you come back here.'

Just play the game, I thought. *Don't say anything you wouldn't normally say. You've got to make him think you're coming back.* And, as if he'd read my mind, he twisted his fingers in my hair and pulled my head towards his as he said, slowly, 'Don't even *think* about not coming back. I will find you.' But the next moment, his arms were wrapped tightly around me and he was whispering into my ear, 'I love you. I don't want to be without you. Just get better and come back to me.'

A few minutes later, I walked down the stairs behind him feeling light-headed and disorientated. I still couldn't believe he was really going to let me get into Steve's car and be driven away. But Steve took my suitcase and dropped it into the boot, my mother almost pushed me on to the back seat, and suddenly we were speeding away from Kas, down the hill and along the road where I'd stood every miserable, lonely, terrifying night for the last six months, and I burst into tears.

Mum reached behind her seat for my hand. 'It's all right now, Sophie,' she said. 'You're safe. It's all over.' I still couldn't believe it, though. Kas had told me so many times that he had people everywhere who were watching me and that he would always know where I was and what I was doing, that I simply didn't believe he'd just let me walk away.

As we drove through northern Italy, I stared blindly through the window of the car, trying to absorb the fact that I was no longer all on my own.

Every few minutes, my phone would ring and Kas would tell me, 'You're my little mouse. I miss you already. I just want you back here with me so that I can kiss you and hug you and touch your hair.' I felt sick, and almost embarrassed for Kas. Did he really think I believed him, after everything he'd done to me? I used to tell myself he loved me, even after he'd forced me to work on the streets and it had become a ridiculous belief. I'd *wanted* to believe it, because unless I could suspend all logic and common sense and convince myself that he cared about me but had to pay off his debt before we could plan a future together, none of it made any sense at all.

Every time Kas phoned me in the car he asked, 'Where are you now?' Each time, I'd tell him that I didn't know, and I could hear the barely suppressed irritation in his voice as he said, 'Well, why don't you ask your mum?' I'd see Mum glance at Steve, who'd name some road or town we'd just passed through and I'd relay the information to Kas. What I didn't know until later, however, was that Kas had given Steve very precise directions for the route he should take to get home, and it was those directions that Steve was using each time he told me where we were. In reality, though, he had been suspicious of Kas's intense interest in our journey and so had taken a different route.

Neither Mum nor Steve asked me anything about what Kas had done to me, and as we drove, Mum held my hand and talked about other things. But I could tell that her cheerfulness was forced and when she looked at me, I could see in her eyes that her heart was breaking.

We stopped that night at a hotel on the Swiss border, which turned out to be a Swiss version of Fawlty Towers. It was run by a couple Steve instantly christened Fraud and Maud, who were barely civil and who served some of the worst food we'd ever tasted. When Steve asked for salad and fries to accompany his steak, Fraud looked at him as though he'd requested caviar and Cristal champagne in a McDonald's, and we only just managed to stop ourselves laughing out loud.

Mum and I did laugh later, though, when we went to the bar and Steve – who's very particular about hygiene – nearly passed out as we watched Fraud cut a slice of lime for his drink, drop it on the floor, pick it up, swill it briefly in some water and slip it into the glass. In fact, that night we laughed until the tears were streaming down our faces and, grumpy and humourless as they were, we were grateful to Fraud and Maud for acting like a safety valve on a pressure cooker and giving us the opportunity to release some of the emotions that had been building up inside us.

As we sat in the bar, talking and laughing, I looked at Mum and then at Steve and felt my heart swell with the love I felt for them. It had been so long since I'd had anyone to talk to that I'd almost forgotten what normality was like and I'd accepted the fact that I would never have anything to laugh about again. I hadn't thought I'd ever feel safe again either, but I came very close to it that evening.

The next morning, we'd been driving for a couple of hours when Mum suddenly said, 'Let's have a singsong!'

'No, Mum. I can't,' I told her. But she insisted.

'Come on,' she said. 'It'll make us feel better. Don't you remember how we always used to sing in the car when you were little?' She turned and took hold of my hand and her voice became quiet as she added, 'Come on, darling. It'll be okay, I promise.'

She started to sing and first Steve joined in and then I did, and she was right: it did make us feel better, and the memory of driving through the mountains between Switzerland and France, singing at the tops of our voices, is one that will always stay with me.

Later that morning, we stopped for coffee at a ski resort, where we sat outside a café in the brilliant sunshine and Mum wondered aloud if one of the people sitting at the table next to ours might be prevailed upon to take our photograph. I was instantly engulfed by panic and I felt my eyes filling with tears as I told her, 'No, Mum. I don't want to have my photo taken. I don't want a picture of me now. Please. Look at the state of me. I look disgusting.'

But Mum just reached across the table, took hold of my hands and said, 'We *will* take a picture, Sophie, and one day we'll look at it and remember this time and we'll be able to talk about it without crying.'

'We won't. That time won't ever come,' I sobbed.

And Mum was crying too as she told me, 'It will, darling. I promise you it will.'

Chapter 13

I don't know how I'd expected to feel when I was at home again, but everything seemed to have changed. In fact, it wasn't so much that *things* were different; it was more that I'd become someone else and so I had a different perception of everything. I'd left home as one person, with particular experiences and views on life, and I'd returned as someone I didn't recognise when I looked in the mirror – someone I felt ashamed to be.

It's hard to explain, but it was as though I didn't know how to act normally anymore, and I didn't seem to fit in anywhere. Although I wanted to, I didn't know how to; I became obsessed with the idea that people might be able to read the thoughts in my head, and then they'd know I was someone who'd done things so disgusting that no decent person would want to be associated with me. I know that if someone told me that what happened to me had happened to them, I'd feel sorry for them and wouldn't blame them for one moment. Even so, I still felt as though it was all somehow my fault.

Perhaps lots of people who've had bad experiences feel like that, and perhaps they feel, as I did, the need to 'get over it' as quickly as possible so that they can pick up the pieces of their old lives and carry on. And perhaps they, too, find that their old lives have been shattered into so many pieces that that's impossible to do. For six months, I'd had to pretend to be Jenna, but now it felt as though I was pretending to be Sophie.

However hard I tried to be 'normal', I remained miserable and kept thinking, *I don't want to be here, but I don't want to be anywhere else. I don't want to be anywhere. I don't fit anywhere. What the hell am I going to do?*

I didn't tell anyone about what had happened in Italy. I knew Mum had decided to give me time and space before asking me about it, and although she was sometimes on the verge of saying something, she always drew back at the last moment.

Kas was still calling me regularly and eventually I told him, 'I'm trying to get well again. I just need to be left alone for a while.' I hadn't really expected him to take any notice, so I was surprised when I didn't hear from him again for the next few days. And then I had a call from someone who said he was Kas's brother.

'Kas has been arrested,' he told me. 'He was picked up by the Italian police when he had a large quantity of cocaine in his car and he's in prison. I need to know if you're coming back.'

I wanted to shout at him, 'Why are you telling me this? This isn't my problem. I don't care about what's happened to Kas. Prison is where he belongs.' But, instead, I tried to sound concerned as I said, 'I'm sorry; I can't go back just now.'

Then I went into the kitchen, filled the kettle to make some tea and stood staring blindly out of the window as I tried to identify the emotion I was feeling. Was it elation? Relief? Disbelief? Pity? Satisfaction? Perhaps it was a mixture of all of them.

I was still standing there when Mum came in and said, 'Are you making tea? Ooh, make one for me, love.' Then she sat down at the kitchen table and told me we needed to talk.

'You need to tell me what happened,' she said. 'I haven't wanted to push you, but I really have to know now.'

'I can't tell you,' I told her. My heart was pounding and the tears that were always just behind my eyes had begun to trickle down my cheeks.

'Yes, you can,' Mum said, reaching for my hand and squeezing it. 'I don't care *what's* happened, Sophie. I don't care what you've done. You will always be my little girl and I will always love you. Nothing can change that, no matter how bad it seems to you. Nothing can change the fact that you're you. But you *have* to tell me. I can't bear to see you so unhappy and not be able to help you.'

So I told her what Kas had made me do and how I'd been so afraid of him and had felt so alone that I'd had to *become* Jenna to be able to do it. I explained how Kas always stood beside me whenever I'd talked to her on the phone, and that although I'd wanted desperately to tell her I wasn't happy, as I was pretending to be, I'd been too ashamed and too brainwashed by Kas to be able to tell her the truth. And as she knelt on the floor beside my chair and held me in her arms, we both began to sob.

Afterwards, when we could talk again, she said, 'I *knew* something was wrong. I could *feel* it. The whole time you were there, I kept telling Steve I didn't believe you'd just walk away from your family, your friends and your job like that. I'd sometimes wake up at 4 or 5 o'clock in the morning and I'd be thinking about you, wondering where you were and if you were okay. I *knew* something bad had happened to you, but I allowed myself to believe what everyone told me – that I was just hurt because we've always had a close relationship and you didn't seem to want to talk to me about anything anymore.'

It turned out that when I phoned Mum from the hospital, she and Steve had already been planning a 'surprise visit' to Italy. Despite the fact that I'd avoided giving her the address of where I was staying – using one excuse after another whenever she asked for it – they'd intended simply to arrive in the area and drive around, knocking on doors if necessary, until they found me. Having lived most of her life in the small, close-knit community of a village, however, I don't think my mum had realised how easy it is for people to 'disappear' in a city suburb, and she certainly hadn't dared to allow herself to consider the possibility that they might eventually have to leave again without me.

Even in her most haunting nightmares, the worst she'd been able to imagine was that Kas wasn't treating me well, and she was completely devastated when I told her the truth. Later, she went upstairs to tell Steve, and he came down, wrapped his arms around me, hugging me so tightly he almost squeezed all the breath out of me, and said, 'Listen, lovey. You're safe, you're well and you're well loved. We're going to look after you and you're going to get through this.'

Mum told my sister, Emily, an abridged version of what I'd told her, and when Emily came into my room, she was sobbing. She threw her arms around me and kept repeating through her tears, 'I'm sorry. I'm *so* sorry, Sophie. I'm *so* sorry.'

That evening, Mum, Steve, Emily and I had a family conference around the kitchen table, at which we agreed not to tell anyone else outside the family, except for Mum's best friend Louise, who knew quite a senior police officer who might know where I could get some help. And it was through Louise's contact that I was put in touch with Robin, who was head of a vice unit and who, quite literally, saved me.

A few days after I'd come home, I'd gone to the hair-dresser and had my hair dyed and cut short. I wanted not to look like Jenna and, perhaps more importantly, I didn't want to have her hair – the hair that Kas and so many other men had touched. Mum had already gone through my suitcase and thrown almost everything away, crying silently while she did it and sobbing when she found the rip in the back of my jacket and the 50-Euro note that was tucked into the lining. I think that was the moment when it all became too real for her to bear, and it hurts me more than anything else to know that, when she goes to bed every night, she has to try to block out of her mind the pictures she must see of what happened to me.

The day after I told her, Mum took me shopping for some new clothes and we were sitting in a coffee shop when I suddenly burst into tears. The look of anguish on her face made me feel even more wretched, and eventually, when I'd calmed down enough to talk, I told her, 'I hate myself. I hate the way I look. I don't want to be in this world anymore. I don't want to have to go on living.'

'Oh, Sophie,' she said, wiping away the tears that were streaming down her own cheeks. Then she took a slow, deep breath and, in a determinedly cheerful voice, told me, 'You look lovely, darling. It's just the way you feel at the moment. It'll get better. I promise it will.'

'Look at me, Mum,' I whispered. 'I'm so skinny and ugly and my clothes are disgusting. I know you want to help me, but it doesn't matter how much money you spend on new clothes for me: nothing will ever look nice on me again. I don't feel nice anymore – I look like a skeleton.'

I tried to pull myself together for my mother's sake and I told her I liked all the clothes she bought me, but I couldn't help thinking, *What's the point? There's no point in my even existing.*

I had other worries too, the main one being that I was in debt. While I was in Italy, the money for the rent on my flat in Leeds had continued to be taken out of my bank account every month – from an overdraft once the account was empty. I hadn't told anyone, and whenever my mother asked about my financial situation, I insisted, 'Everything's fine. Don't worry about anything.' So, of course, she assumed I'd taken care of it. The truth was, though, that being in debt made my anxiety even worse, and I knew I had to get a job as soon as possible so that I could start paying back what I owed to the bank.

Luckily, I found a really good job – on the recommendation of a friend I used to work with – just three weeks after I got home. I knew Mum would have liked me to stay so that she and the other people who loved me could protect me. And, in many respects, that was what I wanted too. But I knew that if I gave in to the temptation to hide myself away, safely cocooned from the real world, I would never be able to build a new life. What was also pushing me away from my family, though, was the fact that I felt as if I was completely different from the girl I used to be. Everything that should have been familiar and comforting seemed strange – although I knew that the only thing that had really changed was me.

So I left my family and moved back into the flat in Leeds. But I couldn't focus. I still felt detached and disconnected, as though I was watching myself from outside my body. I kept thinking, *Pull yourself together. It's over. It's in the past. Move on.* But I couldn't, because everything had changed, and I didn't know *how* to move on. It didn't help that I'd lost most of my friends – as far as they knew, I'd gone to Italy and just stopped phoning them or answering their text messages, which they'd soon given up sending.

I made an appointment at a health clinic and had tests for everything I could think of, and I wept with relief when they told me I didn't have any infections. At least I had that to be thankful for, although it seemed I had little else.

When I had a meeting with Robin, from the vice unit, he asked me, 'Do you understand what's happened to you – that you've been trafficked?' And, strange as it may seem, that was the first time I'd ever thought about it in those terms. Kas had done such a good job of brainwashing me that it had never actually crossed my mind that what he'd done had been entirely calculated and premeditated, and I think, even then, I still wanted to hold on to the belief that, on some level, he loved me.

Over the course of several meetings with Robin, he asked me questions and helped me to see what had happened in a more realistic light. Then, one day, he showed me a photograph and asked, 'Is this him?' I looked at it for a long time before answering, not because I didn't recognise Kas's face immediately, but because I could hear his voice in my head saying, 'If I ever get into trouble because of something you've done, I'll fucking kill you, woman.' But, eventually, I whispered 'Yes.'

'He's wanted here for an attempted shooting,' Robin told me. 'That's why he left the country so abruptly when you first came across him.' He confirmed that Kas was in prison in Italy on drug-related charges and he asked if I wanted him to be prosecuted for what he'd done to me. Just the thought of it made me shake uncontrollably, because I knew that the anger and rages I'd already witnessed would be nothing compared to Kas's vicious fury if he was sent to prison again on the basis of my evidence against him.

'*No!*' I almost shouted at Robin. 'No, I couldn't. I … He'd know it was me. He'd know I'd disobeyed him and then you can't imagine how much trouble I'd be in. He'd kill me – or he'd send someone else to do it. He wouldn't allow me to double-cross him like that. No. Absolutely not.'

'It's all right.' Robin put his hand on my arm. 'No one's going to try to persuade you and I do understand how you feel – it's how everyone feels when they've been through the sort of experiences you've been through. It's what makes my job so difficult, though, and it's the reason why we hardly ever get to the stage of being able to prosecute these bastards. But, believe me, Sophie, I *do* understand,

and no one is going to try to put pressure on you to change your mind.'

I was already afraid that Kas would come looking for me. In fact, I knew it would be one of the first things he'd do as soon as he got out of prison in Italy. It was wrong that he was going to get away with what he'd done to me, and I felt guilty even before someone said to me, shortly after my conversation with Robin, 'If you don't testify, Kas will do the same thing to other people.' But although it was a thought that continued to haunt me for a very long time, I couldn't overcome my fear of him.

Robin insisted there was nothing for me to worry about. 'He won't come back,' he said. 'He's already wanted here, so why would he take that chance? You'll be safe. And if you *are* ever concerned about anything – however silly it might seem – you know how to contact me.' But I was constantly on super-alert, scanning the faces of the people around me, jumping at every sound and continually weighing up the risks – real and imagined – of every situation I was in.

My mother often told me that there was nothing I couldn't talk about to her, but I knew she was wrong and that some things would have upset her too much. So I was grateful when Robin put me in touch with someone who specialised in counselling women who'd been raped. I talked to the counsellor about what had happened and about how it had changed my opinions about myself and my life and everything that used to feel safe and familiar to me. But although she was very nice and the talking did help, I began to feel as though she didn't really understand. It wasn't that what had happened to me was any worse than being raped; it was just that it was different.

Part of the problem was that I couldn't seem to get past the fact that I hadn't tried to escape from Kas. Even in France, when he'd left me on my own for several days, I'd carried on working and doing all the things he'd told me to do. And although I knew that it was because of the fear he'd so carefully and deliberately instilled in me, I still felt as though I'd somehow colluded in what had happened to me – despite knowing, deep down, that nothing could have been further from the truth.

Even before Italy, I hadn't been particularly happy to be the person I was – I had at least my fair share of 'emotional baggage' from my childhood – but I'd have given anything to be that person again now. In just six months, everything had changed and in my mind I wasn't *anyone*; I was in some sort of limbo, without any real sense of my own identity.

I often thought about Erion and how different my life would have been if I'd gone to Albania and married him that summer – which seemed like a lifetime ago. When I think about it now, I realise it might not have worked out well, but I became almost obsessed by regret because I'd let him down and, after Italy, when I felt as though I was completely lost and my future was a dark, empty hole, I was convinced I'd taken the wrong road at that particular crossroads in my life.

I couldn't stop thinking about Erion and one evening I went with my friend Serena to the bar where he used to be the manager. His best friend, Adnan, still worked there and I asked him if he'd heard anything from Erion.

'I just want to know that he's all right,' I said.

Adnan looked at me intently for a moment and then sighed as he answered, 'So you don't know?'

'What do you mean? Know *what*?' I asked, suddenly feeling sick and dreading what he was going to tell me.

'He's back,' Adnan said.

My heart gave a lurch and started to thud against my ribcage. 'How is he?' I asked. 'What's he doing? Where's he working?' My eyes had filled with tears and I felt an almost physical sense of hurt at the thought that he'd come back to England and hadn't got in touch with me.

Adnan shrugged his shoulders and looked away from me. 'I'm sorry, I can't tell you,' he said. 'You really hurt him, you know.'

'I *do* know,' I told Adnan. 'And you have no idea how sorry I am and how much I've always regretted what happened. Is he with someone? Has he met someone else?'

'Please, don't ask me.' Adnan shook his head. 'That's a conversation the two of you need to have. I don't want to hurt you.'

Erion hates me, and I don't blame him, I thought. But I knew I couldn't just walk away and try to forget about him.

'How can we have any conversation at all if you won't tell me where he is?' I asked. 'Please, please help me, Adnan.

You don't know what this means to me. I *have* to talk to Erion.'

'Okay,' Adnan sighed again. 'Give me your phone number and I'll give it to him, but that's all I can do. If he doesn't want to talk to you, you'll just have to accept that.'

A few minutes later, Serena and I walked out of the club and on to the street and I suddenly stopped, clutched her arm and whispered, 'Oh my God, he's there!'

'Who? What is it?' Serena tried to follow my gaze.

'It's Erion. At the pedestrian lights, on the other side of the road,' I said. 'I've *got* to talk to him.'

I don't know if he saw me before he crossed the road, but as soon as he reached the pavement I called out his name. When he turned and looked at me, his eyes were cold and empty and I felt as though someone had stamped on my heart.

'Sorry, love,' he said. 'Do I know you? I think you must have mistaken me for someone you used to know.' And he walked away.

Serena put her arm around my waist and pushed me down to sit on a low brick wall beside the pavement. I felt dazed and sick, but as soon as I could walk again, I scurried home to hide, like an injured animal.

It was a normal reaction for someone who's been badly hurt, I told myself. *He doesn't know why I abandoned him, so of course he's going to want to hurt me in return. But how will I ever be able to explain to him what happened?* So I decided to write him a letter. I didn't tell him about Italy; I just wrote about the pressure I'd been under from all sides after I'd come out of hospital, and how I'd been so confused that I hadn't known what to do. I told him I was sorrier than he could ever imagine and I begged him to give me the chance to explain it to him face to face. And at the end of the letter I wrote my phone number and the words 'It's in your hands.'

Two days later, Erion phoned me and we arranged to meet the following evening. I couldn't concentrate on anything for the rest of the day, and as I lay in bed that night, watching the minutes and hours tick slowly away, I wondered if he would ever be able to forgive me.

I must have looked even paler and more exhausted than normal by the time we met for dinner the next night, and when I asked Erion how he could have said what he said to me at the traffic lights, he answered, 'To be honest, I almost didn't recognise you. I didn't expect to see you. Someone told me you'd gone abroad, so I was taken by surprise when I suddenly came face to face with you. And I was shocked by the way you look. I don't want to hurt your feelings, Sophie, but you're so skinny and your cheeks are so sunken, you look like a heroin addict. And all your beautiful hair has gone! What happened to you? Why do you look so different?'

I couldn't tell him the truth, but he seemed to accept that I didn't want to talk about it in any detail, and as we sat in the restaurant, talking and crying, it felt as though we'd never been apart. I told him how desperately sorry I was that I hadn't gone to Albania as we'd planned, and how I'd wished every single day since then that I could go back and do it all differently. And, from that moment, we were together again.

I don't think I could have shared my life with any other man at that time, but Erion had known me before I'd become Jenna, so to him I was the 'me' I used to be; the 'me' I was trying so hard to find again. I felt safe with him. Sometimes I almost forgot about Italy and sometimes I almost allowed myself to believe I could pick up the life I used to have and start living it again.

Erion and I spent most of our time together. Although he kept his own flat, he came to mine after he finished work almost every night and I told myself it was just like it used to be between us. But I think I knew that wasn't really true and that it was too much to expect anything ever to be the same again. And, as if to confirm those fears, Erion said to me one day, a couple of months after we'd re-met, 'You've changed so much. You're always jumpy and frightened. Why do you always apologise for things you don't need to be sorry about? What do you think I'm going to say or do if you make yourself a drink before you've made one for me? You know I would never even shout at you, let alone hit you. So why do I sometimes feel as though you're afraid of me? You have to tell me what happened to you, Sophie. I need to know, because I can't go on living like this.'

We were having lunch in a café and I wiped the damp sweat from my hands on to my napkin before whispering, 'I don't know *how* to tell you. You're going to hate me. You won't want to be with me anymore.'

Erion reached across the table and I put one of my hands in his.

'Look at me, Sophie,' he said. 'No matter what you tell me, I don't care, because nothing you can say will ever change the way I feel about you. I don't think you've ever understood what you mean to me and how much I love you.'

So, with tears streaming down my face, I told him, and he cried too. And then he said angrily, 'I want to kill him. I hate him. If it had happened to my own sister I don't think it would hurt as much as this does. But I think I knew already – I just needed you to say it. *I'm* here now, though, and no one will ever hurt you again.'

And that was all I wanted, to be with Erion. So why didn't I feel happy?

Perhaps the truth was that although being with Erion made me as contented as it was possible for me to be, despite the fact that I was still having regular sessions with the rape counsellor, I didn't seem to be getting any closer to putting my life back on track. I knew I needed more help, but I didn't know what sort of help or where to find it. And then one day, about six months after I'd come home from Italy, I was searching the internet for *anything* that might hold the answer when I came across a website for a charity called STOP THE TRAFFIK. I went back to it repeatedly over the next couple of days until I finally plucked up the courage to pick up the phone and call the number.

I'd been concentrating so hard on just *doing* it that I hadn't thought about what I was going to say, and when a woman answered the phone, I blurted out, 'I really need help.' The woman's name was Bex, and after talking to her that day, I spoke to her on the phone regularly for five or six months until we finally met in person. The charity STOP THE TRAFFIK doesn't deal with victim support, but Bex talked to me as a friend and as we gradually built up a relationship, I felt as though I'd at last found someone who really understood how I felt.

I'd already been wondering if I might be able to use my own experiences to help other people when Bex asked if I'd be interested in talking to some teenage girls who were living in a children's home and who were thought to be at potential risk from local pimps and traffickers. The prospect of speaking in public about what had happened to me was terrifying, but Bex had been so supportive and so amazing that I was determined not to let her down.

It took three or four weeks for the charity to do various checks into my background to make sure I was who I claimed to be, and then, one afternoon, I walked into a room in London and came face to face with about 10 girls, all of whom looked at me with varying degrees of disinterest, indifference or open hostility. I had to grip the back of a chair to stop myself turning round and bolting back out of the door. I realised I must look like an idiot to them, with my neatly combed hair, carefully applied make-up and smart, work-type clothes, and I could almost hear them thinking, *What the fuck does this skinny little white girl know about our lives and all the crap things that have happened to us?* So I think they were shocked when I told them my story.

Talking about what had happened to me was really difficult. I felt self-conscious and out of my depth and I didn't know where to start. So I just told it from the beginning, sometimes crying, however hard I tried not to, and then feeling a warm sensation spreading throughout my body when I realised that some of the girls were crying too.

When I'd finished, they started firing questions at me and one girl threw her arms around my neck and hugged me as she told me she was certain I was going to do great things in my life – which made me cry again. They were really sweet girls and it suddenly struck me that, just as people might look at me and never imagine I'd worked as a prostitute, they must look at some of those girls and see only the alienation and disaffection that hides their own fears and hurt.

There were two things I wanted to get across to those young girls that day: that they need to be very careful who they trust, and that when bad things happen to you, it *is* possible to pick up the threads of your life – or even to create a new one – and carry on. In reality, however, I was struggling to come to terms with my own inability to trust anyone – particularly men – unless I knew them very well. Even now when I meet someone new, I'm thinking, *Why are you talking to me? What's your real motive? Who are you?* And although I hate being that way, I just can't help it.

Not long after I'd talked to the girls, I was asked by STOP THE TRAFFIK if I'd like to go to a conference and hand a petition to the Under-Secretary-General of the United Nations, Antonio Maria Costa. My immediate reaction was to say no, because I knew I'd be so nervous I'd probably do it all wrong. But then, when I thought about it and about why they'd asked me, I thought that, maybe, if I could overcome my fears and do it, I might be able to use my own experiences to help them achieve something positive.

I hadn't been able to face the prospect of giving evidence against Kas that would have allowed the police to prosecute him and would probably have resulted in him being sent to prison – which is where I knew he deserved to be. But, by doing what I could to support STOP THE TRAFFIK's ongoing campaign to try to raise people's awareness of trafficking in all its various forms, I felt that at least I was doing *something* that might be of benefit to other people.

Despite themselves, the girls at the children's home had been intrigued to know what a well-educated, articulate, 'middle-class', young, white English woman could possibly have to say that might be relevant to them. And I realised that it was exactly those characteristics that might help to change the assumption made by many people that only poor girls from primarily Third World and Eastern European countries are trafficked and that therefore trafficking isn't something that poses a risk to their own daughters or to anyone else they know. So, full of trepidation, I agreed to go to the conference.

I used a false name and the press were asked not to take photographs of me. But it was still all extremely nerve-racking, and on one occasion I nearly had a heart attack when I realised someone was following me down an otherwise deserted corridor at the hotel. I kept glancing over my shoulder and taking deep, slow breaths to stop myself breaking into a run, and I felt like a fool when he turned out to be a security guard – who was making sure no one (else) followed me!

When the time came for me to hand the petition to Antonio Costa, Bex told me, 'If you want to say something to him, do.' So, as I gave him the document, I plucked up all my courage and whispered, 'I'm doing this because it happened to me.' He thanked me, passed the document to a man standing beside him and then, holding both my hands in his, looked directly into my eyes and said, 'God bless you.'

When something bad happens that really changes you, you stop knowing *who* you are. So being part of the delegation to that conference made a huge difference to the way I felt about myself. I'd had to overcome my worst fears on a nightly basis in Italy, but this time I was doing so for a good, positive reason, and the fact that I didn't get it all wrong and mess it up made me think that maybe I wasn't stupid and useless – as Kas had made me think I was.

The conference, with its talks and workshops, was one of the most amazing experiences of my life. I gave a closed talk to a group of girls and although it was still daunting and I was very nervous, I began to have just a little bit more confidence in myself and my abilities. And then I was told that a 10-minute private meeting had been arranged for me with Antonio Costa. I sat waiting outside his room with someone from STOP THE TRAFFIK, feeling sick with nerves and with a thousand questions tumbling around in my head. What would he say to me? What would I talk about? Would he think I was stupid and regret having wasted his time?

But I needn't have been so anxious, because the meeting was amazing. It lasted for a whole hour, during which Antonio Costa asked me questions about what had happened to me and about what I thought the Italian police could have been done differently that might have made me tell them the truth. It's a question to which I still don't know the answer, other than perhaps that they shouldn't treat girls who are working on the streets as though they're worthless scumbags. People who've been trafficked are frightened – for themselves and for their families – and girls being forced to work as prostitutes are often ashamed of what they're doing. So winning their trust – if it happens at all – will be a long, slow process.

For me, apart from the fear I lived with all the time, it was Kas's threat to harm my family that stopped me asking anyone for help. It kept playing over and over again in my head and every time I thought I couldn't carry on any longer, I'd think about my little brothers and about how I wouldn't want to go on living if anything happened to them, and I'd say nothing.

It's hard to imagine what it's like to be totally under someone else's control. I didn't even think to question Kas's authority over me and I believed him completely when he told me, 'My word is law – you must do as I say.' All I *did* think about was trying not to do anything to make him angry. It's a habit I still find difficult to break and I'm forever telling people 'I'm sorry', particularly men, and I'm constantly on the look-out for any sign that might indicate they're cross with me. It's a terrible way to live, and I hate Kas – and perhaps my father, too – for making me like that.

I met Antonio Costa again some while later, when he gave a talk at another conference I went to with STOP THE TRAFFIK. I'd recorded my story and it was played, with my voice disguised, at one of the conference meetings. I was sitting in the audience with my mother, but after a couple of minutes I couldn't bear to listen to it and I had to leave the room. I think part of the reason I found it so distressing was that I didn't want to be there when the recording finished and everyone said, 'Hmm, okay, moving on …' But when Mum came and found me afterwards, she told me there'd been total silence for almost two minutes when the recording ended, and then everyone had started to clap.

'I was so proud of you,' she said, and her eyes were full of tears.

At that moment I saw Antonio Costa walking towards us. He must meet hundreds of people – at least – every month, so I didn't expect him to recognise me, and I'd started to turn away when I felt a hand on my shoulder. He hugged me and then he hugged my mother and said he knew how proud she must be to have such a brave daughter. When he asked me, 'How are your little brothers?' I almost burst into tears at the thought that he'd remembered what I'd told him.

He talked to us for a few minutes and then he hugged me again and said, 'Take care of yourself. Be strong. Be brave.' And I was proud to think that I'd had the opportunity to meet someone so impressive and caring, and so truly interested in the cause he was supporting.

Bex told me recently that someone who works for STOP THE TRAFFIK in Bangladesh had been giving a talk to some schoolchildren there and had told them about a British girl who'd been trafficked. Apparently, they asked a million questions and were amazed and shocked to know that such things occur in Britain because they'd thought they only happened in places like Bangladesh.

'The poor girl,' I said, when Bex finished telling me the story. 'Do you know who she was?' And Bex put her arm around my shoulders, hugged me and laughed as she answered, 'It's *you*, silly! They were talking about *you*!'

And that's when I felt really proud. In fact, it was the most amazing feeling I've ever had, to know that, thousands of miles away in a world I can only imagine, my story might help to keep other girls safe.

Chapter 14

When I came home from Italy, a friend of mine called Jim had helped me to get a job at the company where he worked. It was only temporary, while I got back on my feet and started paying off my overdraft, and after a couple of months I moved on, to work for the company I still work for now.

I'd been in the second job for about four months when Jim phoned me one day and said, 'An email has just been forwarded from your Google account to your old work account here. I think you'd better take a look at it. I'll send it on to you.'

I knew who it was from before I read it. Jim had kept my work account open after I'd left his company so that he could check it from time to time in case there was anything that needed someone's attention, but he closed it shortly after that first email from Kas.

Kas had hacked into my old Google account and found my old work email address. So, when I didn't answer any of the emails he'd sent to the Google account I rarely looked at, he'd sent a message to what he must have assumed was my current work address.

After that first one, emails from him started coming in thick and fast, all of them saying pretty much the same thing – 'You motherfucking police bitch. You have no idea how easy it would be for me to be there in just a few seconds. How dare you talk to the police?' I immediately went into a state of panic. I knew Kas would have read all the emails I'd exchanged with Robin – and sent to an email address that was clearly related to the police – and that he would be raging. Luckily, however, nothing very specific was ever said in those emails, so although Kas would realise I'd been talking to someone, he wouldn't know any of the details.

I didn't answer any of Kas's emails, of course, and then he sent me one saying he would give me back my email account if I told him who I'd been speaking to and exactly what I'd been doing. So I phoned Robin.

'Just continue to keep all the emails and don't respond,' Robin told me. But I couldn't get rid of the feeling that Kas was watching me, and I was terrified at the thought that he was going to come after me, although Robin insisted he wouldn't and tried to reassure me – 'They're just empty threats. Try not to worry.'

A couple of days later, I was at work when I attempted to log on to my email account and found that the password had been changed, which meant that I no longer had access to any of the emails I was being sent by anyone. I was panicking when I phoned Robin again, and this time he said, 'I'm sending someone to pick you up.' Within minutes, two police officers arrived at my office and when I told my boss that an ex-boyfriend was threatening me, she said, 'Do what you have to do. It's fine, just go.'

At the police station, I was told that Kas had been released from prison in Italy and my heart sank. 'What he's doing now is classed as harassment,' one of the policemen said. 'So we need to log it. Unfortunately though, there isn't much we can do unless you agree to press charges. But if anything else happens, you must let us know immediately and we'll send out a rapid response unit.'

As I'd done so many times before, I tried again to imagine what would be involved in pressing charges against Kas. Could it be done here, or would I have to go Italy to do it? But, wherever it took place, how could I possibly stand up in a courtroom and give evidence against him? He'd kill me: he'd see it as the ultimate betrayal and he would never forgive me for it. Even if he was sent to prison, he'd be released one day, and then he'd come after me, which would mean that, for the rest of my life, it would never be over.

I still sometimes think, *He could be doing the same thing to some other girl at this very moment and it's my fault because I didn't do anything to stop him.* But I know I just can't take that step. If I close my eyes, I can *feel* being back in Italy, and the thought of it still fills me with fear. I know what Kas is capable of when he's angry; but I know, too, that the anger I've seen is nothing compared to the way he'd be if I was responsible for his being sent to prison: he wouldn't rest until he'd made me pay for what I'd done. So, however much I might want to stop him, giving evidence against him simply isn't an option.

Although I think Robin always knew I would never testify against Kas, and I think he understood why, he did talk to me about witness protection. But that would have meant having to change my name and my identity and go and live somewhere else, when what I was trying so desperately hard to do was find the identity I'd already lost. Kas changed so much of my life and so much of *me* that having to abandon Sophie Hayes altogether and become someone else would have made it feel as though he'd won.

So I carried on. I couldn't shut down the email account Kas had hacked into because I couldn't get into it myself, but I never used it again. Having given Kas my credit card and PIN number when I left Italy, I had to open a new credit card account and when I gave the guy at customer services my new email address, I told him, at least twice, 'It's really important that you delete the old address and that you only send correspondence to the new address I've given you.' His patience was clearly wearing a bit thin, but he assured me that he'd 'got it' and that it would all be fine

– and then promptly sent a copy of the email containing my new credit card details to the *old* address as well as the new one. Within hours, Kas had sent an email to my new address saying, 'You stupid bitch. Do you really think I want your money? Do you think I'm going to try to steal from you? I don't need your money.' And I had to start the whole process all over again.

I'd periodically check the old email address and find that Kas had sent me links to songs, and messages saying, 'I'm sorry. I love you. I can't stop thinking about you. I can't live my life without you. I need to have you by my side.' As I read each one, I became more convinced than ever that he was crazy and that, somehow, I needed to make him believe I'd vanished off the face of the earth.

I told Erion what was happening and he said, 'Tell Robin. You must tell Robin.' But, for some reason – perhaps because I thought I could handle it myself – I didn't. And then, one day, I got a letter in the post from Kas that said simply, 'I love you. I'm going to come.'

As I stood in the kitchen of my flat, reading the words over and over again and trying to breathe, I was shaking. I felt the same sense of panic and confusion I used to feel when he was shouting and threatening me. It was almost exactly a year since I'd left Italy, and it was only as I stood in my kitchen with his letter in my hand that I realised how stupid I'd been not to move to another flat. I think I'd felt that, because Kas was in prison, I had plenty of time. But now every muscle in my body was tense and I knew I was in real danger.

So, this time, I did tell Robin, and again he tried to reassure me. 'He is *not* going to come here,' he told me. 'The warrant for his arrest for the shooting incident still stands, so he is *not* going to risk going to prison again here. Really Sophie, it's okay. He isn't going to come.'

But, just to be on the safe side, I moved to another flat, and when I checked my old email account a few days later, I found a message from Kas that said, 'I've just been to your apartment. Why are you not there, little mouse? Where are you? I'm here and I need you. I talked to the taxi drivers outside and they said they hadn't seen you for a while and the concierge of your building doesn't know where you've gone. But I won't stop looking until I find you.'

I was sobbing as I read it and I kept glancing over my shoulder, half-expecting to see him standing behind me in the living room of my flat, smiling the small, humourless smile that was so often the first indication I had that I was in trouble. For a while, I just sat there, hunched over the computer keyboard, crying and looking around me from time to time like some crazy woman who can see things no one else can see. Then I picked up my mobile phone and called Robin.

'He isn't here, Sophie,' Robin said, as soon as I'd calmed down enough to listen to him. 'He's probably just looked up your old flat on Google Earth – that's how he knows there's a taxi rank outside it. But he won't come; he'd have to be crazy to take the risk.'

'He *will*,' I whispered, 'because he *is* crazy. He thinks he's invincible, so he has no fear. I know it sounds ridiculous, but I can *feel* him. I *know* he's here and I know he'll find me. What does he have to be afraid of? If he's caught in this country, he'll be deported. So what? Why would he care about that?'

'He *won't* come,' Robin said again. 'You're safe. Try not to worry.'

I did try to take Robin's advice, because I was tired of being afraid of my own shadow. And then, a few days later, I was walking through the city centre on my way to catch a bus home after work when I felt a hand on my shoulder.

I knew immediately it was Kas. Despite the logic of what everyone had been telling me about how foolhardy and dangerous it would be for him to return to England, I knew he didn't play by other people's rules. He believed he was too clever and too important to have to abide by normal laws and regulations, and I'd always known he'd come back for me.

I stopped walking and, for a split-second, stood completely still in the middle of the pavement, aware of nothing except the weight of Kas's hand on my shoulder. The blood was pounding in my ears, making the sounds of the city seem suddenly muffled and distant. The idea flashed through my mind that, instead of turning round to look at Kas, I could start to scream and then, as everyone who was rushing past on their way home from work stopped to stare, Kas might simply disappear into the crowd.

But I knew that even if I did make a scene and draw attention to myself, and even if the people around us didn't ignore me and pretend nothing was happening, Kas would find me again – on another street and on another day. So, with fear flooding through my body, I slowly turned my head and looked into the cold eyes that had haunted my nightmares for so long.

'Sophie, why are you not talking to me?' The regret in his voice was mocking. 'All these years we've known each other. Why are you afraid of me? What's wrong with you, woman? Why are you looking at me as though I'm a terrorist?'

People were surging around us, laughing and talking to each other or speaking earnestly into mobile phones as they hurried home from work. No one noticed a small, pale, frightened young woman or the man who was holding her elbow and speaking quietly into her ear.

I wanted to shake Kas's hand off my arm and scream in his face, 'Leave me alone! It's over. I'm not afraid of you anymore.' But that wasn't true and, in any case, all I could think about was not letting him find out where I worked or lived. Quite apart from being afraid that he might manage to wheedle or bully his way back into my life, I dreaded the thought that he might tell people about me –

about what I'd done in Italy – and then everyone would hate and despise me. I knew I had to pretend to him that everything was normal because, although he knew I'd had contact with the police, if he ever suspected I'd talked to them about him, he'd kill me.

I'd always known he'd find me one day, but I'd pushed the thought to the back of my mind because I was unwilling – or perhaps unable – to deal with it. So I'd never tried to prepare myself for this moment and I was in shock. My heartbeat was echoing loudly in my head and my whole body was shaking. For a moment, I thought my knees were going to give way and I'd fall at Kas's feet on the crowded pavement. But he put his hand under my elbow to support me, digging his fingers into my arm and smiling a cold, menacing smile as he asked, 'What's wrong with you, woman? Why are so scared of me? What do you think I'm going to do to you? I just want to go for a coffee and talk.'

'And I just want to go home,' I shouted – but only silently, in my head.

He put the palm of his hand on my cheek, pushing my face in the direction he wanted me to go, and then he walked beside me to a coffee shop where he bought two coffees and led the way to a table on the pavement outside. As I fumbled in my handbag for my cigarettes and tried to light one, I could feel Kas watching me and I could sense his growing irritation and impatience. I kept swallowing, trying to stop the tears that were filling my eyes from spilling over on to my cheeks, and suddenly Kas reached across the table and snatched the lighter from my shaking hands. I flinched instinctively, expecting him to hit me, but he just looked at me for a moment and then lit my cigarette before asking me again, 'What's the matter with you, woman?'

It was a question he didn't expect me to answer, but if I had, I'd have told him I felt sick and frightened and as though I'd never been away from him. As soon as I saw him, I'd become Jenna again – scared and unable to speak, or even think clearly, while I waited for him to tell me what to do.

He held out his hand, palm upwards, and said, 'Give me your phone.'

'I … I haven't got a phone,' I told him, cringing inwardly at how unlikely that sounded.

'Why are you lying to me?' Kas snapped. 'Why would you be so stupid as to tell me a lie? Give me your bag.'

We were sitting at a table outside a café in the centre of Leeds in broad daylight, surrounded by normal people going about their daily lives, and I was too afraid not to do what Kas told me to do. I handed him my handbag and he pulled out my phone.

'I don't understand you,' he said. 'Why would you not give it to me when I asked? Who do you think you are now – some sort of undercover policewoman?' He looked at me steadily across the table as he said the last word and then asked, 'Why has your behaviour changed?'

And that was when I realised I had to pull myself together and act normally, so that he didn't think I had

266

anything to hide. Incredible as it seems, I don't think the thought had ever really crossed his mind that I might have told anyone about what he'd done to me. Although I didn't consciously realise it at the time, he had a self-assurance and an arrogance bordering on the psychotic; I think he believed whatever he wanted to believe – including, perhaps, that I loved him and wouldn't intentionally do anything to harm him. Or perhaps he simply didn't care what I did – or had done – because he was convinced that he was too clever to be caught.

He typed his number into my phone, rang it, drank a mouthful of his coffee and then leaned back in his chair and said, with a smugly self-satisfied smile, 'So now I have your number.'

'Why are you here?' I asked him. 'What do you want?'

'You sound as though you're not happy to see me,' he said, his face set in an expression of mock hurt. 'Are you not happy that I am here? I thought you loved me, woman.'

I don't even know who you are, I thought. *And I don't think anyone – perhaps not even your own mother – could really love you.*

'You can't know how much I've missed you,' Kas said, flipping from scornful to serious. 'Ah, my little mouse, all I want is for you to be back with me. I don't want you to *do* anything.'

Be smart, the voice in my head told me. *Don't let him beat you. Take what he's taught you about how to stay safe on the streets and use it now.* And I realised that, this time, he was in *my* country and although I didn't think I could actually stand up to him, perhaps I did have a chance of outsmarting him.

'I need to go,' I told him, trying to sound as normal as possible.

'Okay, I'll call you.' He stood up as I pushed back my chair and, putting his hands firmly on my shoulders, kissed me on both cheeks.

I walked home via a long, circuitous route, glancing over my shoulder every few seconds like some terrified hunted animal. But, to my relief, I didn't see him and I began to think that perhaps I *could* stand up to him; perhaps, when he phoned me, I would be able to say, 'I don't want you here; you need to go,' and then he'd know that it was all over between us and he'd leave me alone. It was a fantasy I don't think I ever really believed, because I knew that people like Kas never give up. In his eyes, I belonged to him, and he wasn't going to let me simply walk away.

That night, Erion wasn't planning to come to my flat after he finished work, so, when I finally got home, I locked and bolted the front door and then sat on the floor in the living room with my back against the sofa, smoking cigarettes and trying to focus my mind and think.

Stay calm, I kept telling myself. *Just stay calm and it will all be fine.* But what was I actually going to *do*? I'd already decided not to tell anyone that Kas had come – it was almost as though I thought that if I didn't say anything about it, it wasn't real. I was still very afraid of him, and I was certain no one else knew what he was capable of doing if someone tried to confront him or stand in his way. Most of all, I was afraid that if anyone else did become involved, Kas would carry out the threat he'd made so many times in the past and harm my family. So, ridiculous as it sounds now, by the next day I'd almost managed to convince myself I could handle the situation on my own. Kas didn't know where I lived, and as long as he didn't find out, I was – relatively – safe. And then, a few minutes after I arrived home from work that evening, I received a text message saying, 'I'm outside your flat.'

I threw my phone onto the sofa and began to run from room to room in a frenzied panic, trying to hide anything that related to Erion, the police or STOP THE TRAFFIK. There was a loose floorboard in the bedroom that squeaked every time I trod on it and had irritated me ever since I'd moved in, but I was glad of it now. By tugging at one end, I managed to lift it up just enough to be able to push things underneath it. And then I heard the sound of my phone ringing.

'Don't you dare disrespect me in this way,' Kas shouted as soon as I answered it. 'I know you're in there. Why are you trying to pretend you're not? Let me in *now* or I will get in some other way and break every bone in your body.'

As I walked slowly across the living-room floor to press the buzzer that would release the catch on the door to the street, the voice in my head was screaming, *No! Don't do it! Don't open the door!* But I didn't know what else to do, and a few seconds later, Kas was standing in front of me asking, 'Why did you take so long to answer the door? You're acting as though you have something to hide. Are you trying to hide something from me, woman? Is there something I should be paranoid about, some reason why I should be watching my back? *Why?* Why would you do this to me?'

'I'm not doing *any*thing,' I whispered. 'I'm sorry. I promise.'

He shrugged and said, 'You don't have to be afraid of me. I just want to talk to you, to make sure you're okay. I'll come again tomorrow.'

No! Go away! I don't want you here. I don't want you in my life, I screamed in my head. But I knew that Kas was once again in control.

At work the next day I kept making silly mistakes. It matters to me that I do my job well, and the fact that I couldn't concentrate on anything made me even more anxious and miserable. All I could think about was Kas coming again that evening.

Even after I'd been back in England for a year, I still wasn't in a good place mentally and I didn't have many friends in Leeds. It's difficult to make new friends if you're dreading the moment when they ask what you were doing before you started your current job and you either have to lie to them or tell them, 'Oh, I was working on the streets in Italy.' And you don't really expect other people to like you when you hate everything about yourself.

There were days when I'd get up, do my make-up and my hair, get dressed and look in the mirror and think, *No*. Then I'd take off my make-up, wash my hair again and change my clothes – sometimes repeating the same wretched, frustrating process again and again until finally deciding not to go out at all.

I became obsessed with the way I looked, and convinced that people were looking at me thinking, *What a mess!* It still happens now, although not as often or as intensely. But at that time there were many days when I couldn't leave the flat because I couldn't find myself. When I looked in the mirror, I didn't recognise the girl who was looking back at me, and sometimes I'd just stand there thinking, *Who am I?*

Inevitably, Erion and I were drifting apart, and although we were still 'together', he didn't stay at my flat as often as he used to. He'd ask me, 'Why do you always listen to such sad music? It's difficult to be with someone who's always so unhappy.' And I knew that he was right, because it can't be easy to live with someone who hates herself as much I did and who's paranoid about everything. The slightest noise or sudden movement would make me jump, and Erion would look sad as he told me, 'I feel as though you think I'm going to hit you. It hurts me because you know I would never do that.'

I was confused and unsure about every aspect of my life and perhaps that's at least partly why I made the foolish decision to try to stand up to Kas on my own. I don't know how he'd managed to follow me home without my seeing him. Maybe he'd got someone else to do it, and maybe what he'd told me so often was true and he *did* have people everywhere, watching to make sure I did what he told me to do.

That evening, when I pressed the buzzer to open the outside door and he walked up the stairs to my flat, I didn't pretend I was glad to see him. And he must have noticed the fear and resentment in my face because he asked me, 'Why are you acting this way? What have I ever done to you to make you afraid of me?'

I almost laughed. I wanted to shout at him, 'Are you insane? Have you lost your mind so completely that you don't know what you've done to me?' But I said nothing, and he told me I was 'ridiculous' and that my behaviour was 'pathetic', and then he said, 'No one knows I'm here. Do you have any idea how easy it would be for me to take a pillow and press it down on your face until there is no breath left in your body? No one would ever know what had happened. So remember that, and think very carefully before you disrespect me.'

He came again the next night, this time to tell me a crazy story, which I knew was almost totally untrue.

'I need something from you,' he said, and my heart started to beat so fast I couldn't breathe. 'I need you to go back to work. I've found a place in Liverpool. It's a house, so you won't have to be out on the streets.' He said it as though he was offering me some kindness or favour, and I began to feel as though I was trapped in a surreal nightmare. 'It'll be easy this time. You'll be in a house and you speak the language, so it's easy money. Remember, little mouse, you're a goldmine. You'll be brilliant.'

'I can't,' I blurted out at last. 'I *can't* do it.'

'Come on,' Kas cajoled. 'You'll be fine. You can still do your day job. I'm not asking you to give it up. You can work Friday and Saturday nights – just two nights a week.'

Then his mood changed from coaxing to angry and he shouted, 'Why are you making such a big deal out of this? All I'm asking you to do is open your legs and have sex for two nights a week. Why are you looking at me like that? I'm not asking you to kill someone. I'm not even asking you to break the law. What's wrong with you, woman?'

For the first time for as long as I could remember, I felt a sense of determination and resolve. It wasn't anything very substantial, but it was just enough to enable me to dare to look him in the eye and say, 'I *won't* do it.' And then, suddenly, I didn't care what he did to me, because I knew I would rather he killed me than that he forced me back into a life of fear, loneliness and shame.

'Do you think I'm *asking* you?' he barked at me, and I could almost see the rage flaring up inside him like a flame. 'Don't you realise how easy it would be for me to get you out of this country if I wanted to? How simple it would be to inject you with a drug that made you unconscious, throw you into the back of a lorry and have you out of England before anyone even noticed you were missing.'

He'd said much the same thing to me before, and I knew that it was true.

'Think about it,' he told me. 'I'm not an unreasonable man, so I'll give you some time to decide which way you'd rather do this. I'll be back tomorrow.' Then he opened the front door and walked out of the flat, and I curled up on the sofa and wept.

Kas didn't come back the next night or the night after that, although he phoned several times to remind me he was watching me. And by the time I heard Erion's key turn in the lock of my front door late one night, I'd realised I couldn't fight Kas on my own and I told him what had happened.

'Right, I'm phoning your mum,' Erion said immediately. 'Why on earth didn't you tell me about this before? Why do you shut me out so that I can't help you? Why do you shut *everyone* out when it's clear you need help?'

'You can't phone her now,' I told him tearfully. 'It's two o'clock in the morning. She can't do anything at this time of night except worry. Please, *please*, Erion, let me tell her when I think the moment is right.'

So he agreed to wait and although he fell asleep with his arms wrapped round me, I knew that by shutting him out, I'd risked losing him.

I had to go to a work meeting in London the next day, and as I sat on the train, staring blindly at the world speeding past the window, I felt as though I was trapped in a vortex, spinning faster and faster and waiting for the moment when it would spew me out and I'd have to try to land on my feet.

It was about 11.30 that morning when my phone buzzed and Robin's number flashed up on the screen. The meeting had already started, so I muttered an apology, said something about having to take 'this important call' and walked out of the room into the hallway.

'I've just had a conference call with your mum and Erion,' Robin told me. 'Erion's told us everything. *Jesus*, Sophie, why didn't you tell someone sooner? You could have come to me, you know. Why didn't you phone me?'

'I thought I could manage it on my own,' I said, and the words sounded stupid, even to me.

'Then you clearly haven't understood just what you're messing with,' Robin sighed, echoing the words Erion had used when I'd told him what had happened. 'You can have no idea what you're involved with or the danger you're in, otherwise you'd know that you can't deal with this on your own. I do understand, though,' he added more gently. 'I know that you're so deeply involved in it that you're unable to take that step backwards that would allow you to see the situation as anyone else might see it. But the thing you have to understand, Sophie, is that you will never win against a man like that. He doesn't play by the rules that govern what normal people do – people like you and me. He makes up his own rules, which are based on just one immutable fact: no one and nothing matters to him except himself and what *he* wants. You have to let me take charge of this now.'

It was what I'd often thought about Kas myself and I realised, with relief, that Robin was right. Until that moment, I'd thought *I* was the only person who under-stood what Kas was capable of and how his megalomania and delusions of self-importance guided all his actions. But the truth was that I was so afraid of him, I was the very last person in the world who should be trying to stand up against him.

As soon as I finishing speaking to Robin, I got a text message from Erion, saying, 'I'm sorry. But even if you never speak to me again for the rest of your life, I had to do this. You may hate me, but I did it for you.' I wiped my sleeve through the tears that were streaming down my face, and then my phone rang again.

I could tell as soon as I heard my mother's voice that she was almost frantic with worry. She told me later that she'll never forget Erion's phone call that day or how devastated and heartbroken he sounded, and that she'll always be grateful to him for making the decision to tell her. She'd phoned Robin immediately, and in their conference call a few minutes later, Erion had told them, 'I realise now that I've seen him in a coffee shop and I know I can't just stand by and do nothing. If no one else can stop him, I'm going to do it myself.'

'I understand how you feel, but, please, don't do anything,' Robin had said. 'We haven't been able to take any action while he was in Italy and while Sophie didn't want to press charges against him, but it's out of her hands now that he's here. She's going to have to leave Leeds for a while to give me time to work something out.'

Somehow, I managed to get through the rest of the day in London and when I arrived back in Leeds the following afternoon, my mother met me at my flat. Within two hours we'd cleared everything out of it. My boss already knew something was going on and when I went into work to tell her I had to leave, she was brilliant. 'Just go,' she told me. 'Do what you have to do and I'll sort everything out here. I'm sure we can find a way for you to work from home.' So, once again, I left my life in Leeds, this time to go home with my mother and wait to hear from Robin.

A long time later, Erion told me that a couple of days after I'd gone home, he'd been walking through the city centre with a friend when they'd been stopped by a man who was a friend of Erion's friend and who introduced the man *he* was with as Kas. Erion was horrified, but he'd been forced to shake Kas's hand – for the sake of appearances, so that he didn't give away the fact that he knew who he was – and he'd had to look away so that Kas wouldn't see the anger and hatred in his eyes. I don't suppose Kas would have noticed, though, because I'm sure he was still bliss-fully unaware that I'd told anyone what he'd done to me or that he had come back to Leeds to find me.

Erion often went to a coffee shop that was popular with Albanians and other Eastern Europeans, which is where he heard that Kas had become friendly with a long-distance lorry driver. 'It isn't just a chance friendship,' Erion told my mother. 'He's planning to take Sophie. However afraid she is, she still has no idea of the danger she's really in – she can't deal with someone like that on her own.'

A couple of days later, Robin rang me and said, 'We need to get you out of the country for a few days, so we've arranged for you to stay at a "safe house" in Germany, with some relatives of someone who works for STOP THE TRAFFIK. You need to disappear. Change your phone number and don't write anything on any internet site – which means not even logging on to MySpace or Facebook, or anything similar. Close your accounts if necessary. Shut everything down.'

So I did as he told me, and 48 hours later, I was on a plane, being swept along on a tidal wave and wondering where on earth it was going to take me.

Chapter 15

The German couple I stayed with were very kind to me. I shopped and cooked with the wife and went out on my own for long bike rides in the countryside, and when I'd been there for three days, Robin phoned and said, 'You don't need to worry anymore. We've got him.'

I burst into tears and all the fear and anxiety that had been building up inside me for so long exploded out of me like the air rushing out of a pricked balloon. At first, all I could say was 'Thank you. Thank you.' But eventually I calmed down enough for Robin to be able to tell me what had happened.

Apparently, after I'd left Leeds, the police had stopped and searched Kas in an area frequented by drug dealers. He'd been carrying several passports, all issued in different countries in different names and all with his photograph, and when he was arrested and fingerprinted, his existing arrest warrant for the attempted shooting had been flagged up.

I returned to England a week later and, not long afterwards, Kas was sentenced to a year in prison, to be followed by deportation to Albania.

It felt as though the hand that had been gripping my throat for so long had been removed and I could breathe again. I didn't have to be afraid of my own shadow anymore, and I didn't have to look over my shoulder all the time, although I don't know if I'll ever manage to break that habit completely. Even now, I jump at every loud noise and flinch if anyone raises a hand near me for any reason.

Even after Kas had gone to prison, I'd still sometimes search the internet for any mention of his name or for any sign that might indicate he was active again – partly because finding nothing allowed me to go to bed at night feeling secure. And then, one day just before Christmas, about eight months after he'd gone to prison, I looked on the social networking site he used to use and found that the 'last active in' date had changed from May to December. I stared at the screen, unable to make any sense of what I was reading, and although I told myself that it was a mistake and it wasn't possible for him to have logged on to his website just a few days earlier, I phoned Robin in a panic.

He tried to reassure me by telling me, 'He's in prison, Sophie. So it can't have been him.'

'He *isn't* in prison,' I insisted, knowing that I sounded paranoid and hysterical. 'I'm telling you, Robin. He's out.'

'Okay,' Robin said. 'Just to put your mind at rest, I'll make some enquiries and then I'll call you back.'

And it turned out that I was right. After serving just over half his sentence, Kas had been deported back to Albania. I knew that I could no longer afford to feel safe and that if he wanted to risk coming back for me, he'd find a way. All I could do was hope he'd decide I wasn't worth it.

I still think about him for some reason on most days, and I sometimes wonder if he's doing the same thing to some other poor girl, and pray that he isn't. People tell me they understand why I can't bring myself to give evidence against him and that they wouldn't expect anyone in my position to put themselves through such a terrible ordeal, particularly without any guarantee that he'd be convicted. But I still feel really guilty about it, and I wish I was braver.

Moving back to live with my mother, stepfather and sister that summer was the best thing I could possibly have done. I spent almost all my time with Emily, and I know that, without her and Mum's support, I'd never have got anywhere close to being back on track and able to do 'normal' things again. My boss at work continued to be brilliant too, and to organise things so that I could carry on working from home. And then, not long after I came home from Germany, I accepted a transfer to the London office and the opportunity to start again somewhere new.

Erion and I saw each other occasionally, but, over the years since we first met and fell in love, our relationship had been stretched to its limits and beyond. So I suppose it was inevitable that, eventually, it would start to show signs of strain, and I think I knew even before Erion said anything to me that he could no longer cope.

He was crying as he told me, 'No matter what happens, I will always be here for you if you need me.' And he's kept his word, coming to visit me for a wonderful weekend after I'd moved to London and phoning me from time to time to ask how I am. He sent me a text message last Christmas saying, 'I miss you. I wish we could turn back time.' And I wish that too.

I wish things had turned out differently and that I'd gone to Albania to marry Erion when I had the chance, because losing him is the one thing for which I know I'll never forgive myself. But it's too late. You can't move forward with your life if you're constantly looking over your shoulder – for whatever reason – and I know that what I'm wishing for is something that just isn't there anymore. Too much has happened since we were first together; I've changed too much and I'm no longer the person I was when we met. But I know that Erion is the only man who has ever truly loved me, and the fact that I lost him will always make me sad.

Occasionally, I check my old email account and a few months ago I found an email from Kas in which he said, 'I love you. I miss you. I hope you're happy.' Not very long ago, reading it would have sent me into a downward spiral of fear and panic, but now I feel almost sorry for him because I know he won't ever get even close to understanding or experiencing what love really is.

If I came to face to face with Kas now, I'd still be frightened of him, but only because I've been conditioned to fear him. I'm stronger than I used to be and I'm not alone anymore, so I know he can't hurt me, and I think I'd have the strength to say 'Leave me alone.'

When he came back to Leeds for me, I knew he was coming. It sounds melodramatic, but I could *feel* it. Even so, I was blind-sided and I wasn't ready to deal with him. I don't think he'll come again, though. His only real concern in life is to protect himself, and coming here now would be risking too much – and for what?

I used to be so desperate to believe he loved me that I almost convinced myself he did, even though his every word and action proved otherwise. But, against all the odds, I survived those months in Italy and now I'm determined not to live in fear, and particularly not to allow a man like Kas to rule my life by making me afraid. I'm stronger now and I refuse to think, *I can't do this because of him*. If I *am* ever forced to deal with him, I'll meet him head on and try to stand my ground against him.

People who know about what happened to me say, 'My God, how do you deal with things like that?' And the only answer I can give them is, 'You *have* to – there's no choice.' I do worry, particularly about things like doing my work well, and I always put as much effort as I possibly can into everything I do to try to ensure that I don't fail and that people don't think badly of me – which is perhaps still more important to me than it should be. But I try to remember to be proud of the obstacles I've overcome.

What Kas did to me opened my eyes to the terrible things some people are capable of doing to others. Working with STOP THE TRAFFIK is helping me to make something positive out of what I'd thought was a totally and irretrievably negative experience, and I want to use that experience to try to help other people who haven't been as fortunate as, ultimately, I was and to help raise awareness about people trafficking.

It's easy to dismiss girls who work on the streets as deadbeats or drug addicts without ever thinking about why they're working as prostitutes. And the truth is that many of them have been trafficked and they work long, exhausting, miserable, soul-destroying hours for men who are cruel and violent. They're constantly afraid, not just because of what might be done to them if they don't do what they're told, but also because of the very real threats that are made against their families and the people they love.

What kind of person does that to another human being?

At the moment, except when I'm giving talks for STOP THE TRAFFIK, I don't tell people about what happened to me. I just want to be Sophie. And that means that I sometimes feel as though I'm living a double life, although I prefer to think that I'm living *my* life – Sophie's life – and that I've left Jenna behind me in the past. Not telling people can make things difficult, though – for example, when I over-react to something and can't explain why, such as the time someone at work fired a toy gun at me and I fell on the floor with my hands over my head, screaming.

I'm not brave enough yet to stand up and face people and speak openly about my experiences, but I know one day – when the time is right – I *will* be.

Although it's probably difficult for anyone to guess what happened by looking at me, I still carry it with me and I still find it difficult to distinguish feelings. I broke up with a boyfriend recently after we'd been together for about a year, and the only thing that surprised me was the fact that he'd stayed with me for as long as he did. Whenever he told me he loved me, I'd ask him 'Why? How do you know?' – which isn't really a response designed to make romance blossom!

I still have to try really hard sometimes not to wish certain things were different – that I'd gone to Albania that summer and married Erion, that I'd never met Kas, that Steve had been my real dad, and that my own father had loved me. My brother Jason said that when he told our father about Kas and what had happened to me in Italy, Dad said, 'Let's go and break his fucking legs.' But he never even phoned me to find out how I was, and although I'd like to believe he said it, I think it was just my brother's way of trying to make me feel better.

As well as the psychological scars Kas left me with, his physical violence towards me has caused long-term back and neck problems. It was recently discovered that the headaches I keep getting are due to severe nerve damage, for which I have to have regular treatment. They start abruptly, without any warning, and are excruciatingly painful, so I've had to curtail some aspects of what would otherwise be my normal life. Worst of all, though, is the fact that they're a constant reminder of Kas's brutality towards me and of his almost-daily vicious attacks.

On the positive side, I think I am finally learning to accept that some things can't be changed and there's no point wasting your life wishing they could. I often feel as though I'm climbing a ladder, at the top of which are all the good things I hope I'll have one day – including a strong sense of self-esteem and the ability to accept love without question and to live at peace with myself. At the moment I'm only a few rungs up that ladder, and I can't even see the top of it yet. But I know that if I keep climbing, I'll get there in the end, however long it takes me.

A Note from Sophie's Mother

When Sophie rang that day and asked about Auntie Linda, I thought my heart was going to stop. I'd known all along there was something wrong, from the moment she rang to say she wasn't coming home and that she was going to stay in Italy with that man. I'd never met him and I had no reason to believe he didn't treat her well. But I know my daughter, and there was something in her voice that made alarms bells start to ring in my head.

Sophie is a beautiful young woman – that's a fact, as well as being my own personal opinion as her mother – and not only physically, but in terms of her character too. She and her sister and brothers have always stuck together and supported each other and I'm very proud of them all. I'm desperately sorry they were hurt so badly by their father and that, because of the way he treated them, they needed each other's support. I couldn't love and admire them more for the amazing adults they've all become.

In Sophie's slight, delicately fragile-looking body beats the heart of one of the most courageous young women you are ever likely to meet. I admire her enormously: for having survived such an unspeakable ordeal at the hands of that man, for picking up the shattered pieces of her life and struggling to create a new one, and for her determination to try to ensure that something good and positive comes out of the terrible things that happened to her.

For me and for my husband, Steve – Sophie's stepdad – that journey to Italy was the most difficult of our lives. In fact, before Sophie rang me from the hospital, we'd been planning to pay her a surprise visit. Steve had suggested it because he knew how worried I was about her and he thought it would put my mind at rest. The problem was, though, that Sophie had never given me an address. Every time I asked, she'd make some excuse – they were going to be away for a while, or that man was about to move to another flat and she'd let me have the new address when they were settled. But we thought we'd just be able to turn up and find her.

We live in a small village, where, if you asked enough people, you'd eventually find someone who knew whoever you were looking for. And, naively, I'd thought it would be the same when we got to Italy. We knew what area Sophie was living in, so we thought that if we went there and asked around, someone would know her – as I say, she's pretty and *vivacious and most people remember her once they've seen her. When I think about that now, though, I still feel sick with anxiety, because I realise we'd never have found her. Like so many people who are trafficked, she'd have disappeared without trace and none of us would ever have seen her again.*

I know that I came, quite literally, within just a few minutes of losing my daughter forever. From what the police told us later and from what I saw of that man myself, I'm convinced he was planning to take her out of the hospital that day and sell her on to someone else. Can you imagine how that feels – to know that your intelligent, kind, lovely daughter came within a hair's breadth of being sold, like some object or animal, and of being lost forever to the people who love her and who she loves? I try not to think about it – or about all the other women, men and children who suffer every day all over the world because some people have something so badly wrong with them they think it's all right to treat other human beings in that way.

When we arrived at the hospital in Italy, that man was already there and I wanted to kill him. Sophie was almost unrecognisable. She was so thin she looked like a frail, vulnerable child, and although her expression was blank, her eyes were like two enormous dark pools of fear. I couldn't look at that man, although when I did glance at him, I noticed that he didn't look at all as I'd imagined. He was probably in his mid to late twenties, tall and powerfully built, but with a receding hairline, a pronounced gap between his front teeth and an unattractive face. He wasn't nice-looking at all, although I suppose partly what I was seeing was the beast below the surface.

He tried to charm us, and I could see that Sophie was terrified in case we upset him and made him suspicious about why we'd really come, but I couldn't make eye contact with him. And because I didn't kiss him goodbye when we left – the thought makes me sick to my stomach – he told Sophie later, 'I don't want to know your mother; she'll never see our children,' which made me wonder if he was crazy. Did he really believe – or think she believed – that once we'd got her away from him, she was going to go back and live with him, share his life and have his children? I suppose he must have done, otherwise I don't think he'd have let her go, but it's completely beyond my comprehension and I still can't decide whether he was actually mentally deranged or simply pure evil personified.

It was clear he was furious when the people at the hospital ignored him, turning their backs on him and refusing to let him be involved in their discussion with us. When Sophie and I went into the doctor's office, I spoke on the phone to someone at the embassy who told us, 'Just take her home. Don't worry about anything at the hospital.' And when the nurse put her arms around me and hugged me silently, I knew she knew what had happened to my daughter.

As we drove behind his BMW to the horrible, sleazy hotel where Sophie had been staying, he tried to lose us by weaving and darting through the traffic. Fortunately, Steve was more than a match for any tricks he could pull – we'd found

Sophie, against all the odds, and he wasn't about to lose her now.

Later, as the three of us drove through Italy, Switzerland and France – travelling via a tortuously indirect route in case he had people watching out for our car – Sophie whispered into her phone every time he called her, telling him she loved him and missed him. But her voice was anxious and placating and her eyes were full of fear, so that it took all my will-power not to snatch the phone from her hand and throw it through the open window. It was as though someone had taken away our Sophie and replaced her with a smaller, frightened, empty replica of the bright, lively, feisty girl she'd always been, and it broke my heart to look at her.

It was clear to us then and for the next few weeks at home that, quite apart from the relentless physical abuse Sophie had suffered at the hands of that man, she had been completely brainwashed and terrified by him. She tried to hide the bruises that were all over her body, but I knew they would gradually fade – although she still has physical health problems as a result of his beatings – and that it was the psychological damage that was going to be the really difficult thing for her to deal with.

A few days after we'd returned to England, we tried to take Sophie's phone away from her, to stop her talking to that man, but she became so hysterical we had to give it back again. Although we knew that she was confused and lost in the world she used to know so well, what we didn't know until later was that he was trying to lure her back to Italy by *threatening to hurt her sister and brothers, and that she had been so brainwashed by him, she was seriously considering doing as he said.*

Although Sophie's father was never physically violent towards her, she learned when she was a child to avoid being the focus of his anger and aggressive temper by doing exactly what he told her to do. It broke my heart at the time, but I think that it was her ability to read her father's moods and to do as she was told that saved her life in Italy. It's remarkable really, because she isn't a tough girl at all; she's very gentle and kind and, although she's quiet, she feels things deeply.

For a while when Sophie came home, I was worried for her and about what her future would hold, but I know now that not only will she survive, but she'll also continue to put her experiences to good use. And I'm very proud of her for that.

To people like that man, everyone else's life is cheap, and I have no doubt at all that he'd have got rid of Sophie – one way or another – if she'd caused him any trouble. I pray that none of us will ever set eyes on him again. I hope he's serving a long prison sentence somewhere – preferably in some country where prison conditions are bleakly harsh. I hate him, and all the other men (and women) like him.

Perhaps some people will find it hard to understand why Sophie didn't try to escape or tell the police what was happening to her. But, if they do, it's probably because most of us have never experienced real, paralysing fear – the sort that blows apart your established mindset and all the things you thought you knew about life, and then freezes your mind so that the only thing you can think about is getting through the next few minutes, the next hour and, if you're really lucky, the next day.

I think many people assume that most of the girls who work as prostitutes do so willingly, for one reason or another, so I think what every man needs to consider before he picks up a girl on the streets is whether he would like his own daughter or sister to be standing in her place. Because whatever people would like to believe, the vast majority of those girls would give almost anything to be somewhere else, doing something else. The truth is that although they may be smiling, they're frightened. Many of them have been brainwashed and intimidated into doing what they're doing and they are completely without hope of finding any way out of the miserable lives they've been forced into by circumstances or by evil, low-life, self-serving people like the man who stole my daughter.

There's no shame in what Sophie did – quite the reverse in fact, because something unimaginably terrible happened to her and instead of giving up and allowing it to beat her, she became determined to live the life she chooses to live and to try to help other people by working with Stop the Traffik in their attempts to raise awareness of what's happening on a very significant scale to all sorts of people from all sorts of walks of life around the world.

I loved Sophie and I was proud of her before she went to Italy, and I love her and am even more proud of her now. I *know she's struggled because she feels she isn't the same person anymore, and that's true – but only because the person she is now is stronger and more beautiful in every way than the girl who put her trust in a man who was nice to her and who came close to losing everything, including her life, because of it.*

Sophie loves her stepfather, and their relationship is important to both of them, so I know that, in time, she'll learn to trust other men too. And that's what I hope for her: that she'll find someone worthy of her and of her love and trust.

A Note from Robin

My first impressions of Sophie were that she was intelligent, well spoken and frightened. Whenever I spoke to her she was always polite, and she was clearly extremely grateful for any time I spent listening to her or acting on what she told me. But she was fairly unusual in comparison with many other victims of trafficking in that she was prepared to talk to the police at all. Most people are too scared to come forward, for various reasons. For example, victims from abroad are often wary in case the police might be corrupt, or they think we won't be interested in what's happened to them. And sometimes they're afraid because they believe they've committed an offence by working as prostitutes – albeit against their will.

However, the police in the UK are far more au fait with trafficking than they were even just a few years ago, and our

295

actions are led by what's best for the victims and for their safety. That's why I didn't try to push Sophie into making an official complaint against the man who trafficked her – although without it there couldn't be any prosecution.

Sophie was terrified when her trafficker came back to England and got in touch with her. But it was his emails and the contact he made with her – and the fact that she eventually told us about them – that ultimately enabled us to trace him, despite all his different aliases, identities and false documentation. And when he was sent to prison by the courts for another, earlier offence, it meant that Sophie had at least a few months during which she could feel safe, which is when she started to build a new life for herself.

Although I'd already had experience of talking to the victims of trafficking before I met Sophie, she was the first British national I'd come across who'd been trafficked abroad. In fact, I haven't encountered another one since then, although I know there must be a lot more out there.

I believe strongly that the more publicity there is about trafficking and the more knowledge people have about it, the better equipped we'll be to fight it. Anything that results in just one extra person being rescued from repeated beatings and rape is worthwhile, which is why I was so pleased to know that Sophie is trying to create something positive out of her own horrendous experience by working with STOP THE TRAFFIK and by writing a book about her ordeal.

When I was in Romania recently, working on a case that involved Romanians being trafficked to the UK, I spoke to the stepfather of a victim whom we'd rescued. Since the time she was a baby, the man had brought his stepdaughter up as though she were his own child, and when I met him he burst into tears, thanking me and my colleagues again and again for making her safe.

He also kept asking us to go to his house before we returned to the UK. So the next day we arrived in a small, immensely poor village, where the family greeted us like royalty and ushered us into the victim's younger sister's bedroom – which, it turned out, was the only room in the house with a heater.

While we ate the small cakes and drank the fizzy drink they'd bought for us – at a cost that must have seemed like a fortune to a family as poor as they were – the stepfather told us how, when his stepdaughter was young, he and his wife had decided that for the next ten years they would eat only one meal a day so that they could afford to send her to school on a bus.

Meeting that family was a deeply humbling experience, and it was part of the reason why I hope to be able to continue to investigate trafficking and try to rescue as many victims as possible.

In many ways, Sophie didn't fit the 'normal' mould of the victims of trafficking I usually come across in my work. Although she was in the same age range – from 17 to mid-30s – they're usually from very poor families who live in villages on the outskirts of towns, predominantly in Hungary, the Czech Republic, Slovakia and Romania. Some have been assessed as having very low IQs and I've even encountered some who were brought up in Romanian orphanages.

There are various circumstances that lead to us rescuing people who've been trafficked: some manage to escape with the help of a client in a brothel; some use someone else's phone to send a text message home saying, simply, 'Help' – and then their families contact the local police, who alert Interpol; and sometimes we're contacted by members of the public, or by sex workers or brothel receptionists who've become concerned about girls after one of our Harm Reduction Visits, when we tell them the signs to look out for.

Since our unit was set up a few years ago, every trafficking case that has led to a court hearing has resulted in the offender being found guilty and receiving a custodial sentence. In fact, in one recent case in England following the rescue of six victims, the main offender was sentenced to 21 years in prison.

But although it's gratifying to see that sort of sentence being handed out, my motivation for doing the work I do is connected more with seeing the faces of victims when we rescue them, when they know that they're able to speak to their families and they begin to realise they're safe and we're going to help them. In order to achieve that outcome it's important that people know about these crimes. So I hope that as many people as possible will read Sophie's story, because only by being aware of what's going on in our own neighbourhoods will we be able to succeed in the fight against human trafficking.

Robin is a Detective Constable working for the UK Sexual Crime Unit.

A Note from Bex

The first time I spoke to Sophie was when she contacted STOP THE TRAFFIK, the charity I work for, and told me, 'I need help.' I don't think she knew at the time what she was looking for – perhaps she just needed to talk to someone who would understand what had happened to her. But, as it transpired, it was the start of a relationship that I think has proved mutually beneficial. Getting to know Sophie and hearing about her experiences – and now reading her book – have given us a deeper understanding of what it's really like for someone to be trafficked.

I'm glad that Sophie has been able to tell her story, not only because I think people need to hear it, but also because it's her justice.

I know that when people hear a story like Sophie's some of them ask, 'Why did she stay? If that happened to me, I'd just go to the police.' But the men who groom girls for trafficking are clever. They're good at identifying a particular girl's issues so that they can use these to manipulate and control her. And the reality is that it isn't so easy to take action to protect yourself when you're the victim of someone completely ruthless and violent who makes you believe – as Sophie's trafficker did – that you can't trust anyone else at all.

Sophie has so much going for her in terms of her education, intelligence, a good career, and family and friends who love her. So when you realise that it was impossible for her to tell the police – or even her mother, to whom she's very close – what was happening to her, you wonder what hope there is for people who haven't started from such a strong place and who don't have anyone to turn to.

When I'm asked what makes someone vulnerable to trafficking, I talk about poverty, political instability, natural disasters, lack of education and employment opportunities – although none of those issues affected Sophie. Then, when I've listed all these factors, I'll say, 'And there's love as well.' But Sophie's trafficker was her best friend, which, in a way, made her even more vulnerable, because whereas you can sometimes feel insecure in love, you generally trust your best friend. And he was unusual, too, in terms of the length of time he groomed her. So one of the reasons Sophie's story is so important is because it breaks down all the usual stereotypes.

300

The focus of our work at STOP THE TRAFFIK – which is largely staffed by volunteers – is communities. Everyone is associated with some kind of community – whether it's a social-networking community, a university community or a business community – and when someone contacts us and asks what they can do to help prevent trafficking we ask them: Who do you know? What networks are you part of and who can you tell about trafficking? Before they can do anything, people need to know that the problem exists, so the first significant action to be taken is to raise awareness. One of the communities we are all part of is our geographical community, our neighbourhood – and, as people are trafficked from one community into another, if everyone in these two communities understood what trafficking is, maybe we'd be able to prevent it happening, or could at least respond appropriately to people who've been trafficked into our community.

Our aims are therefore to help create communities in which it's more difficult for traffickers to operate and to hide themselves and their victims and, as well as raising awareness of trafficking, there are a myriad ways of doing that. One of the things we're currently working on with other agencies is putting together training for teachers so that they can talk to children about grooming and pimping, and make them aware of the need to protect themselves and their friends.

There are always likely to be signs that someone has been trafficked from a community. For example, as was the case for Sophie, they might have rented a flat but not be living in it and/or have suddenly and uncharacteristically left a job without contacting their work colleagues, friends or members of their family. And in the community they've been trafficked into, they might be the unhappy-looking foreign girl who moves into a flat with a man, and who comes and goes at odd times of the day and night.

Of course, as well as being alert to the tell-tale signs of trafficking, anyone who suspects that someone in their community has been trafficked needs to know what to do about it. So something else that concerns us at STOP THE TRAFFIK is who might see what's happening and who might be the right person to step in and intervene in a way that's appropriate in a particular case, because what would work for one person might be completely the wrong thing to do for another.

For example, in some countries you wouldn't go to the police, because they don't have the training to deal with the issues involved – perhaps they don't understand trafficking or they haven't established a victim-centred approach. In the UK, however, you can contact your local police station or Human Trafficking Centre, or any of the services listed below. And you don't need to be afraid of getting it wrong: the police won't mind if it turns out that you've made a mistake.

STOP THE TRAFFIK works closely with the police in several countries, as well as with the United Nations and the Serious Organised Crime Agency (SOCA) in the UK. One of the things we need in order to be able to make it harder for traffickers to function is community information. No one can be truly invisible. Even people who have been trafficked for domestic servitude and who rarely set foot outside the place where they work must sometimes be seen by someone.

People know what's going on in their community and there's always someone who knows who's responsible when a serious crime is committed. Which is why, by raising awareness of trafficking, we hope that we'll be able to encourage people to realise that they need to release the information they have and help us to protect those who are vulnerable.

Sophie's life was taken away from her almost overnight, and what she experienced during the next six months could have destroyed her. But although what happened to her will be with her for ever, her recovery has been extraordinary. After an ordeal like Sophie's, many people would want to stay close to home, where they feel safer. But Sophie chose to move to another city and into a house with flatmates she didn't know. It was a choice that had nothing to do with escaping – she has a loving mother, family and friends; it was all about creating something new. And that's exactly what she's managed so successfully to achieve.

It was very hard for Sophie for the first year or two after she came home. But she finally feels safer. Her networks are stronger, the man who trafficked her has been in prison (so she knows he isn't invincible after all), she has a very good job and she's worked hard to develop some great new friendships. And now that she's tasted life again, she won't give it up easily.

Sophie Hayes

If we can all work together, perhaps more men, women and children who've been trafficked will be able to feel the same.

Bex Keer
STOP THE TRAFFIK

STOP THE TRAFFIK

Men, women and children are being exploited by force or by trickery all around the world. They are victims of human trafficking, a global crime by means of which criminals earn vast amounts of money from abusing the human rights of vulnerable individuals. Every community in the world is affected, whether people are being trafficked from, through or into that community, or whether the goods and services available in that community are produced using the forced labour of human-trafficking victims.

Due to the nature of this crime, it is very difficult to obtain reliable, up-to-date information about how many people are affected.

The International Labour Organization estimates that there are at least 12.3 million people in forced labour worldwide. Of these, approximately 2.5 million are victims of human trafficking and half are under the age of eighteen. 43 per cent of victims are trafficked for commercial sexual exploitation, of which 98 per cent are female. 32 per cent of victims are trafficked for economic exploitation, of which 56 per cent are female. The remaining 25 per cent of victims are exploited in more than one way: for domestic servitude, street crime, drug cultivation, benefit fraud, forced marriage or other forms of abuse.

The nature of trafficking also varies from region to region. For example, 90 per cent of all human trafficking in the Middle East is for economic exploitation, but in Europe only 25 per cent is for this purpose.

People are trafficked for profit. It is estimated that the global profits generated from the work of the world's 2.5 million forced labourers who have been trafficked amount to US$31.6 billion per year. This represents an annual average of US$13,000 per victim. Profits from trafficking are far higher in industrial countries than in non-industrial countries, rivalling those of major global companies. Spending on efforts to tackle human trafficking by governments and charities pales by comparison, however, which is why local communities have such a key role to play.

More information about human trafficking can be found on the website www.stopthetraffik.org.

Simon Chorley
UK Coordinator
STOP THE TRAFFIK

Contact Details

Sophie Hayes Foundation
www.sophiehayesfoundation.org
The Sophie Hayes Foundation works to increase awareness
and raise funds to assist the NGOs that work so hard to
combat human trafficking and to support survivors of this
terrible crime.

Police emergency – 999 If you think someone is in
   imminent danger, you *must* call 999. Do not try to
   intervene yourself.
CrimeStoppers – 0800 555 111 If you want to report
   something anonymously.
Salvation Army – 020 7367 4500 If you are a victim in
   need of support.

UK Human Trafficking Centre
Telephone: 0114 2523891
For advice and information.

STOP THE TRAFFIK
Telephone: +44 (0)207 921 4258
Email: info@stopthetraffic.org
Website: www.stopthetraffik.org
For information about community action and resources. This is also a good first port of call for anyone who wants information and advice.

William Wilberforce Trust
Telephone: +44 (0)207 052 0336
Email: info@williamwilberforcetrust.org.uk
Website: www.williamwilberforcetrust.org.uk
Provides frontline practical support for women coming out of situations of trafficking. Through the volunteer-led project it equips and empowers these women to choose their futures, free from abuse, and to use their voices to change society and bring hope to other women who have gone through similar experiences.